MARRIED TO *Amazement*

Also by Kathleen Coskran

The High Price of Everything, Minnesota Voices Project Winner in 1987 and winner of a Minnesota Book Award in 1988

Tanzania on Tuesday: Writing by American Women Abroad, co-editor, winner of a Minnesota Book Award in 1989

An Inn Near Kyoto: Writing by American Women Abroad, co-editor

Kathleen Coskran's conversational writing style, encyclopedic memory and keen eye for detail make her a wonderful storyteller. *Married to Amazement: Saying Yes,* her memoir, is the best story she'll ever tell. Her experiences as mother, grandmother, spouse, daughter, sister, Peace Corps volunteer, educator, writer, pilgrim and adventurer spirit us around the world from Georgia and Minnesota to Ethiopia, Kenya, Nepal, Colombia, Europe and China. At each stop she finds the common threads that bind us together—love, sorrow, hope, disappointment—in what she calls "the great human adventure on earth."

—William Hershey: author of *Taking the Plunge into Ethiopia: Tales of a Peace Corps Volunteer;* former Washington correspondent for the *Akron Beacon Journal* and former Statehouse Bureau Chief for the *Akron Beacon Journal* and the *Dayton Daily News.*

Kathleen Coskran is a captivating storyteller. Her tales lodge in the reader like keepsake memories of the wonders and complexities of the world to be savored again and again. From working in Ethiopia, Kenya, China, Nepal, and home in Minnesota, she celebrates the truly amazing diversity of the world from birth to death through the complexity of every unfolding life.

—Julie Neraas, educator, spiritual director, and author.

Writing with great style and heart, Kathleen Coskran takes us through the many countries and adventures of her life inspired by her Peace Corps days in Ethiopia and the unfolding gift of family. She ends with "Learning from the Young," interviews with her grandchildren which shed light on our larger story, the story of which we are all a part.

—John Coyne, author of 29 fiction and non-fiction books

MARRIED TO
Amazement
A MEMOIR

KATHLEEN COSKRAN

A PEACE CORPS WRITERS BOOK
2025
OAKLAND, CALIFORNIA

Married to Amazement: A Memoir
A Peace Corps Writers Book—an imprint of Peace Corps Worldwide
Copyright © 1968 to 2025 by Kathleen Coskran
All rights reserved.

Printed in the United States of America
by Peace Corps Writers of Oakland, California.

No part of this book may be used or reproduced in any manner whatsoever without written permission except in the case of brief quotations contained in critical articles or reviews. For more information, contact peacecorpsworldwide@gmail.com. Peace Corps Writers and the Peace Corps Writers colophon are trademarks of PeaceCorpsWorldwide.org.

ISBN-13: 978-1-950444-81-6
A Library of Congress Control Number has been assigned to this title.
To obtain cataloging information, please contact the Library of Congress.
First Peace Corps Writers Edition, May, 2025

Cover and book design by Mayfly book design
Cover Photo: *The path to Brighter Futures Children's Home, Bistechap, Nepal,* by Kathleen Coskran.

This book is dedicated to my grandchildren

Kilian, Cailyn, Sienna, Núria, Beck, Cassie, Sa'ada, Senat, Arwa, Owen, Audrey, and Ellie

Contents

Amazement: an Introduction xiii
   So This Is Paris 1

Family 13
   An Either/Or Proposal 15
   Sick in Kisumu 21
   Safari Surprise 27
   Our Beautiful Boy 33
   The Lucky Family 39
   Proxy 43
   First Grandchild 61

Follow the Child 65
   Transition 67
   Straining for the Light 71
   Discovery of the Child 77
   Poetry by Heart 83
   Higher Calling 85

Second Time Around 87

Matatu 89
Mwembe's Woman 91
Brighter Futures 117
Second Time Around 123

Encounters 129

Dragonflies 131
Hi, Robert Frost 133
Return 137
Dilla 139
Teacher 145
The Art of Walking 151
Reading Poetry 167
Circus of the Damned 171

When Death Comes 179

The Gift 181
Close Encounters 187
A Simple Man 195
The Ultimate Tiny House 203

The Larger Circle 209

Learning from the Young 211

Afterword 217

The Third Goal 217
The Dragonfly 221
Acknowledgements 223

And what do I risk to tell you this, which is all I know?
Love yourself. Then forget it. Then, love the world.

—Mary Oliver in "To Begin With, the Sweet Grass"

Amazement: An Introduction

I am delighted to be old, really old, *old old*, eighty-one years old. Delighted because I am still here, reasonably healthy, mobile and intact, with only a few bits of implanted metal holding me together, and I am still just me. I have heard that wisdom comes with age, but I don't buy that.

Experience—yes. There are things I would never do again, things I will never *have* to do again (or tell anyone that I did), things I have learned, and quite a lot I still want to do . . . but wisdom? That's a stretch for me—not going to happen.

But amazement, wonder, and gratitude have shown up again and again, from the miraculous birth of my children and then the even more amazing arrival of grandchildren and technological innovations that no futurist ever predicted. (Did anybody ever think we would be taking pictures with that heavy black thing with a receiver and rotary dial—the telephone?) Or having a meeting over zoom? Hmmm, a zoom meeting must mean an extremely quick and effective gathering that we *zoom* through, zoom a verb not a noun, certainly not an adjective. (And those technological developments have people of a certain age dependent on their children and grandchildren to explain it to them—the *young* are the technologically wise ones.) As Mary Oliver wrote in *When Death Comes*, "When it's over, I want to say all my life / I was a bride married to amazement . . . I don't want to end up simply having visited this world." [1]

Exactly.

※

I hadn't thought much about amazement when I joined the Peace Corps in 1965 and was assigned to Ethiopia, a country I had to look up in the encyclopedia . . . but I *was* amazed to learn that this African country was a 3,000-year-old kingdom, one of the world's oldest countries. That's where the gift, the conscious gift, of amazement began for me, that combination of surprise, discovery, knowledge, and pleasure. Amazement expands the world when you become "the bridegroom taking the world into [your] arms."[2]

The first essay in this celebration of amazement begins there, in Ethiopia, where I learned not just to embrace the unknown, but to savor it and to know that my life was deepened and expanded by living the daily, ordinary life of a new teacher more than 7500 miles from home.

The penultimate section focuses on that final human experience, death, approached quite differently by the three people closest to me: My mother, who never complained nor spoke about the final passage as it became inevitable, my good-hearted father, who had so much to live for that he couldn't believe he was actually dying, and my brother, who lived a life of curiosity and wonder at the natural world and was an active presence to his dying and preparation for death. He told his hospice nurse that his goal was "a good death," which he created for himself and those of us who loved him. It was his final accomplishment, the last act of an amazing life.

The last section, "The Larger Circle," was inspired by poet Wendell Berry's poem of that name and physicist Aaron Freeman's advice:

---

1. Oliver, Mary. "When Death Comes," *New and Selected Poems*, Volume I. Beacon Press, 1992.
2. Ibid.

"You want a physicist to speak at your funeral. You want the physicist to talk to your grieving family about the conservation of energy, so they will understand that your energy has not died . . . According to the law of the conservation of energy, not a bit of you is gone; you're just less orderly."[3] That larger circle includes and encompasses us all, every creature that ever lived, including you and me . . . which *is* amazing.

---

3. Short speech on NPR, "All Things Considered" by physicist Aaron Freeman, June 1, 2005.

So This is Paris

The year Detroit burned[4] I taught English and algebra in Dilla, Ethiopia. There were four of us *ferenjis*[5] in Dilla that year. Doug, from Michigan, saved all the clippings from *The Christian Science Monitor* that his mother sent him about the riots and brought them out whenever a student asked him about his country.

He would unfold the dark pictures of burning buildings and say, "This is my home."

"He reads too much," Dick said. Dick didn't have time to read. He never missed a soccer, basketball, or volleyball game with the students or a chance to spend an hour at *Negussie Beit*, the only bar in Dilla with a refrigerator.

Our students called Claudie their mother because she stayed at school long after the sun went down to talk to them, help them with their homework, or give them advice. The day she bandaged Hamid's infected arm, he asked if she had ever been a Scout.

---

4. In August 1966, police officers confronted and arrested three men for "loitering" near the AAYM (Afro-American Youth Movement) headquarters, sparking four days of conflict between police and the Black community.

5. *Ferengi* is the word shouted at foreigners, that originates from the Persian word "farang" which originally referred to Franks and later expanded to include all Westerners.

"Yes, I was," she said.

"I thought so, Miss, because you are always prepared."

The seventy-five students in my homeroom, 7-A, were proud of me because I called the roll from memory every morning, Addiswork Bekele to Zeudi Memedin. They called us all the Peace *Corpse*.

Most days after school the four of us walked down to the post office on a clay road that sucked at our shoes in the rainy season and streaked our clothes with dust in the dry season. We passed old ladies shouting *"ferengi"* at us, stepped around sheep and goats crossing the main drag, stopped to admire the professional mourners in a funeral procession, paused so the water man, rolling his massive barrel up the hill from the river, wouldn't lose momentum. As the barrel rumbled past and the mourners took up their ululations again, a gutsy six-year-old ran up, tagged Dick, then dashed back to his friends, Dick would spread his arms wide and say, "So *this* is Paris."

*

School began with a chalk shortage that year. Students often asked for the chalk at the end of class. I used every piece down to the last grain—there was none to spare. I also kept the fingernails on my right hand short to get full use out of every piece and to avoid spine-raising screeches on the blackboard. One day, I had used a piece of blue chalk down to a shadow of color. Zelalem, in my sixth grade English class, asked me for it, so I gave him this blue nothing and told him to save it for me. Like the man and his two talents, Zelalem gave me back twice as much chalk the next day. Somewhere he had found a grain of white chalk the same size as my spent blue piece. When I walked in the next morning, he opened his hand and presented me with two specks of chalk for the class. The pieces were so small that he would have lost them if he had put them down anywhere. He must have held the chalk in his hand all night.

※

A few weeks later we were talking about capitalization. Each student was giving me an example of a word that is always capitalized, easy words, such as Ethiopia, Dilla, their own name. I hesitated when I reached Nasin Shaffi. Nasin was the slowest kid in the school; he was teased by the other students and scored zero on every quiz I gave. I worried about embarrassing him again, and when it was his turn to suggest a proper noun, he stood up and mumbled something.

"What?" I asked.

Nasin repeated what he had said, in clear, full tones: "Dag Hammerskjold."

※

On St. Patrick's Day I explained my Irish heritage to 7-A and the importance of the day. Abraham, the biggest troublemaker in the school, raised his hand. "We should go outside, Madam, to celebrate your holiday."

"Yes, yes, good idea," somebody said.

"No, that's not necessary," I said, but the students were already moving toward the door.

Tsegay Mekonnen, the class monitor, stepped to the door to stop them. "No," he said. "It is her holy day. We must have five minutes of silent prayer." Not what I had in mind, but they all went back to their seats and bowed their heads.

※

The first time I saw Tsegay in action, he was stepping across a desk in the back of the room with a switch in his hand to hit another boy who was talking out of turn. It was my first day at Atse Dawit School.

"Hey, stop that. What do you think you're doing?" I said.

"No, Madam. Is okay. He is the monitor."

Tsegay stood against the back wall with his arms laced across his blue shirt watching me advance on him. "I am monitor," he said.

"Who says you are monitor?" I asked. I was familiar with the monitor system of class discipline, didn't like it, and didn't want it in my classroom.

Tsegay shrugged and the other students again confirmed that he was the class monitor. I said the monitor should be elected by the class and proceeded to explain the democratic process, the duties of the monitor (no switches allowed), and the responsibilities of the students to each other, to the monitor, and to their teachers; then I took nominations from the floor. They elected Ayelu Hailu.

Because not everybody was able to start school when they were six years old, the age range of my seventh graders was twelve to twenty-two. Ayelu was a slight twelve-year-old, the smallest boy in the class, meek and overwhelmed by his sudden elevation to high office. The students snickered when I announced the election results. I insisted that they respect Ayelu, affirmed my confidence in him, and said that his word would be law regarding matters of discipline. Ayelu took a deep breath, realigned his shoulders, and strutted to the back of the room where he could keep an eye on everybody. I resumed the math lesson.

He lasted four days.

The second time around they elected Hamid. I was pleased. Most of the students had the chiseled features, slight frame, and red-brown skin of the highland Ethiopian, but Hamid's family had emigrated from the far west. He was an imposing figure, 6 feet tall and pure black. But his service as monitor was a day shorter than Ayelu's, and I didn't understand why he was unsuccessful until later, when I heard him called "the black one" and *shankalla* (slave).

I told the students that I was furious with them for electing two successive monitors whom they refused to respect.

"Tsegay is our monitor, Madam."

And so he was. He became an invaluable advisor for me, an inside operator. "Bekele is not sick, Madam. He have woman." Or "Kebede hates Alemayu. Better move him." When I remember that class now, Tsegay's handsome face is always in the middle of the back row, his eyes roving over the rows of students. By the end of the year, I had convinced him to give up the switch, but I noticed faint lines in his forehead and a wariness in his eyes when he confronted certain students.

※

We had electricity from 6 p.m. to 12 p.m. most nights. I planned lessons and graded papers when the lights were on. After midnight, I sat up with a book pressed flat against the table, reading by candlelight in the dark kitchen. The only noise was the occasional cough of a hyena passing in the street and the *sitz* of insects flying into the flame. I blew the specks of their parts out of the fold as I turned the pages. I savored each word of those delicious books. I also read *TIME* cover to cover every week, including the sports and business sections. I read the listings of books published on the flyleaf of Penguin library editions. I read the small print of ads in the English language *Ethiopian Herald*, a weekly newspaper.

I even read *The Fanny Farmer Cookbook* cover to cover. I knew nothing about cooking. I was raised by a mother who claimed that packaged foods were the most profound advancement of the twentieth century. She relied heavily on frozen fish sticks, chicken pot pies, and canned asparagus. All her cookbooks had "quick" or "jiffy" in the title.

There was no processed food in Dilla. We could dependably buy only onions, bananas, and meat. Sometimes there were cabbage and carrots. Once there was eggplant. We could also get rice, but there were insects in it. You had to dump it on the table and pull the rice into a bowl in your lap while killing the bugs and pushing them off to the side. Salt and spices were measured into cones of old newspaper, weighed, and sold. The egg man delivered his tiny eggs wrapped in banana leaves, thirty for a dollar Ethi. We bought oatmeal, canned margarine, tuna fish, powdered milk, and tins of vegetables when we went to Addis Ababa. The tuna fish and tinned vegetables were so precious that we allowed ourselves to eat them only on special occasions. In the end, we left two cans of beets, one of green beans, and one of corn for the next volunteers. We wrote them a long letter, introducing them to our town, our students, and our canned vegetables.

※

There was only one female Ethiopian teacher at Atse Dawit whom we called *Weizerite—Miss*. Claudie told her we wanted to learn to cook Ethiopian food, so she came by one afternoon with eight newspaper cones of different spices and told us to grind each spice separately, then spread it in the sun to dry, then grind each again, separately, spread it in the sun to dry again, then grind it, dry it, grind it a fourth time and spread it in the sun to dry. *Then* we were to mix them together in such and such proportions, sauté the onions for two hours until all the water was out of them, then add the spice mixture. "Meanwhile...," she said, and started chopping a kilo of mutton into cubes the size of her thumb nail. I had stopped listening. My heritage of jiffy cooking made me inadequate for the task, but Claudie wrote it all down. We never cooked anything with the *Weizerite's* spices. Our last week in Dilla, we sifted the spices into *birillas*, the bulb-shaped glasses used for drinking honey *tej*, sealed them with wax, and took them home to America. They still line the top shelf of the highest cabinet in my kitchen.

※

One day the Amhara bankers in town, Ato Mahari and Ato Hamare, dropped by for tea and invited the four of us on a picnic.

"Terrific," I said. "Do you want us to bring something?"

"Yes, of course, you women will cook," Ato Mahari said, "but we will hunt first. We will get partridges and lesser kudu and have a picnic in the grand style." Mahari and Hamare were as *ferenji* as we were in Dilla where the people were either Sidominia or Derasse. (The two of them, the four of us, plus Ato Aberra, a big man on the Coffee Board, and Ato Bekele, the school superintendent, formed the middle class of Dilla. A handful of local landowners and Negussie and Mohammed, who owned bars, were the upper class.) Mahari's and Hamare's wives were shy, elegant women who didn't eat with us when we were invited to their houses, and they wouldn't be going with us on the grand picnic.

Claudie and I couldn't find a single reference to lesser kudu in *Fanny Farmer*. We approached Dick and Doug for help. They were sitting on their front porch with Tafesse, the third-grade-teacher who shared the house with them. Dick had just come back from a soccer game and had a towel wrapped around his head to soak up the sweat. Doug was reading. Tafesse was smoking a cigarette.

"They expect us to cook," I said. "You have to help us."

Dick rubbed his head with the towel. Tafesse stubbed out his cigarette and grinned. Doug looked up from his book.

"You're the best cook," Claudie said to Doug. "You cook the kudu."

"Can't," he said. "Would be insulting to Mahari and Hamare. We are guests in their country and must obey their customs."

"It is clearly women's work," Dick said.

Even Tafesse laughed when I said, "Come on, you guys. This is serious."

They wouldn't help us, so Claudie and I concocted a salad that we loosely referred to as coleslaw, bought bread from Montenari's, and took the Weizerite's spices.

The day of the picnic, Mahari did kill two of the tiny antelope known as lesser kudu. He skinned and bled them for roasting while Hamare built the fire and Claudie and I paced nervously.

"We've got these spices," I said, but Mahari waved us off and roasted the delicate kudu parts without the spices. We had our grand picnic in a grove of flat-topped acacia trees under the watchful eyes of local Derasse children. Later, Dick and Mahari played with Mahari's revolvers as if they were cap guns. In my pictures from that day, there is a series of shots of the two of them facing off with the guns in their pockets, Western gunslinger style. Dick has a towel wrapped around his head and his hand on his hip, ready to draw; Mahari is doubled over, laughing at the crazy American.

※

Even the most remote town in Ethiopia had one or two Italian men who married Ethiopian women after World War II and stayed on to bake bread or make pasta. In Dilla, Montenari ran a small bar and had the only bakery. There had been a second Italian who ran the town generator, but he died shortly before we arrived, so Montenari was alone. One Friday, Doug and I stopped at his bar just before midnight. The place was empty, he was ready to close, but he still had coffee, so he poured us some, and himself some, and he sat with us. He spoke no English and only a little Amharic, and we spoke no Italian, so the three of us sat there in silence, this old Italian and two young Americans, drinking espresso in the middle of Ethiopia. At midnight, when the lights went out, we rose to go, but Montenari held his hand up and shook his head. He wanted us to stay. He brought candles and more coffee. We sat with him a while longer and listened to the hyenas who began their eerie whoops as soon as the electricity shut off every night.

When we finally left Montenari's to walk back to our houses in the dark, Doug took my hand. "Dick is right," he said. "Paris is like this."

※

Ato Aberra, the Coffee Board man, loved to play cards with us, especially after we taught him Hearts. He was a born capitalist and never accepted the idea that in Hearts the *low* scorer wins—he was a twenty-five-point man. I ran into him at the bank one day, surrounded by huge boxes of money. Each box held $600 Ethi in five-cent pieces—1,800 coins per box. Aberra explained that he was on his way out to buy coffee and the Derasse wouldn't accept paper money or any coin larger than a five-cent piece. "You can have any box you can carry away by yourself," he said.

※

On St. Mikhel's Day,[6] the school and all the businesses closed because there was a St. Mikhel's church near Dilla. The day began with all the Coptic Christians in town congregating on the soccer field in front of the school. The priests, dressed in their brightest velvets, gathered at one end of the field surrounded by acolytes holding red, purple, and gold umbrellas over their holy heads and swinging incense burners in front of them. The town officials flanked them on the left. The teachers, including the four Peace Corps Volunteers in the front row, sat on the right. The speeches and invocations lasted two hours: most of the ceremony was in Ge'ez, the religious language of the Coptic Church. Only the priests knew what was going on. After the speeches, we proceeded to the church. Everybody went: students, women with small children, farmers, bar owners, prostitutes, and the four *ferenjis*. It was a 10-kilometer walk; beggars lined both sides of the roads and paths all the way to St. Mikhel's and swelled in numbers at the gates to the church courtyard. Lepers without fingers or toes or with parts of their faces wasted away, men with elephantiasis (one or both of their legs swollen like a tree trunk), legless men, emaciated women with children with distended bellies, women with open, oozing sores; the lame, the poor, the insane were all trotted out for the procession. Giving to the poor was part of every holy ritual.

※

We could get BBC, Voice of America, Radio Moscow, Radio Deutschville, and sometimes Radio Vatican in Dilla. Abraham interrupted my algebra class one day. "Why do you shoot Negroes in bars?" he said.

---

6. St. Michael's Day

"And burn your cities?" someone else asked. They listened to the radio too.

Lester Maddox, the restaurateur who sold axe handles to keep African Americans out of his Pickwick Restaurant, was elected governor of my home state that November. Tsegay Mekonnen asked me about the new governor of Georgia and axe handles.

"The democratic process doesn't always work the way you think it ought to," I said.

Tsegay nodded. He already knew that.

※

The week before we left Dilla for good, I had a party for the seventy-five students in 7-A. I made popcorn and bought a stock of bananas for refreshments, but I was stumped when it came to entertainment. Music was out. Our radio reception was too poor; I had no record player. The house was small—two twelve-foot-by-twelve-foot rooms—but I thought the kids could mingle and talk, eat a banana, and extend the party out into the yard. But they wouldn't go outside. They filled one room, two and three deep, crushed against the four walls. I distributed the popcorn, organized pin the tail on the donkey in the other room, and tried to engage them in conversation, but they were politely monosyllabic. The easy conversation of the classroom was silenced by the solemnity of the occasion. The party in my house had made them mute.

Finally, Tsegay said, "Madam, can we dance?"

"Yes, of course. But where and to what music?" There was a square yard of open floor at best.

"Don't worry, Miss." Tsegay issued instructions to several of the students, took Addiswork's scarf, and stepped to the center of the room. Yakob found an empty patch of wall and drummed the mud plaster with his five fingers and the heel of his hand. Tsegay began moving in small circles in the middle of the room. The girls sang. Bekele clapped his hands in counterpoint to Yakob's drumming. Tsegay moved faster, holding the scarf taut between his hands, over his head, behind his back, then dropping an end, following it. Everybody sang, punctuating their songs with shouts and ululations.

They were of different ethnic groups, different religions, but they knew what to do. When Tsegay finished, Addiswork took her scarf and stepped to the center of the room. Everybody sang and drummed as she began to move. The party was a success.

※

On our last day, we got up early to catch the first bus to Addis Ababa. When I opened the back door in the predawn light to go to the outhouse, I discovered Tsegay, Hamid, Zeudi, Ayelu, Mulugetta, Nasin, Zelalen, and many others waiting in the yard. Dozens of students had gathered in the dark so they wouldn't miss our departure. They hovered around our two houses as we packed. They trailed us down the dirt roads of Dilla for the last time. They insisted on carrying our things to the bus. Tsegay presented me with a basket his mother made. "So her name will be known in your country," he said. We got on the bus and waved until we couldn't see them anymore.

The road out of Dilla is a steep climb, and the bus slowed almost to a stop by the last switchback. There is a point where the whole town is as visible as a map—four parallel streets up from the river, bisected by paths, with the school at the high end and the bus park, where clumps of our kids still waved, at the low end of town. The four of us craned toward the windows for a last look.

"So this was Paris," Dick said softly.

"No," I said, "this was better."

Family

✿

I may not be wise, but experience has shown me how amazingly lucky I am because of my wonderful, imperfect family; brought together in multiple, sometimes unexpected, ways.

An Either/Or Proposal

It has been nearly sixty years since the phone call. It was the middle of the day; he was calling from his office in Washington, D.C. "Hi," Chuck said. "Look, I'm on my way to a meeting, so I've only got a minute, but I just checked my calendar, and I could get married on either January thirteenth or the twentieth."

In the years since that startling announcement, I've rehearsed better responses than the one I eventually gave. I wish I'd at least had the wit to say, "Oh, really! Married to whom?"

We'd met eighteen months earlier as Peace Corps Volunteers assigned to the same summer vaccination project. Local men trained as practical nurses picked us up every morning to take us to a different village market. There one of them stood on the back of the Land Rover, announced our presence, and swarms of people descended on us with their arms extended to receive the magic shot. We vaccinated 8,000 people that month. On days when there was no market, we galloped on horseback across the green hills of central Ethiopia. It was wonderful.

At the end of the summer, we returned to our teaching jobs, his in Addis Ababa, mine in Dilla, a twelve-hour bus ride south of the capital. I saw him when I went to Addis, he visited me once in Dilla, and we traveled together over spring break. It was a Peace Corps romance, but when our tour was over the following June, he left immediately for the job in Washington; I set out with my roommate Claudie to see the rest of the world. I didn't expect to see him again.

※

Claudie and I had planned to fly to Khartoum and follow the Nile River north, but our departure was two weeks after the 1967 Six-Day War and our passports had been stamped *Not valid for travel in Sudan, Egypt, Syria, Lebanon, Israel, Iraq, Jordan, Kuwait, UAR, Yemen, or Saudi Arabia*. As a result, we flew to Tehran, began our trek there and traveled west by bus for the next four months.

※

I'd been home three weeks when he called the day before Thanksgiving. I'd seen him twice in those three weeks, but we had not spoken about marriage or even made declarations of love. I didn't know him well enough then to know that when he gets an idea, particularly what he thinks is a really *good* idea, he acts immediately. He was busy the day he called, on his way to a meeting, he said, with no time for conversation, discussion, or words of affection. He'd had a good idea, identified consecutive weekends when he was available for implementation, and made time for a call to seal the deal.

I, on the other hand, was standing in my parents' kitchen in Atlanta, in jeans and a sweatshirt, with no calendar to check, still reeling from the shock of being back in the United States. I had given some thought to looking for a job in D.C., to get to know him better in case something developed, but actual marriage had never occurred to me.

But he was waiting, probably less impatiently than in this telling—or maybe not. I know him well now and decisiveness and action are his gifts; patience is not. The question was clear. It was not a *yes* or *no* question. It was a *when* question, an *either/or* question, and he'd generously offered me *two* possibilities nearly eight weeks in the future.

"January thirteenth or the twentieth?" he said again.

I was stunned by the question, but in simplifying the proposal, he had made it easy, offering a choice, not *if* but *when*, and so I responded, "The twentieth." It was farther away; it would give me time to think, to worry, to process—plenty of time. I could feel good about being decisive, but I was queasy at the implication.

Well, it was two months away.

※

It was my fault. Months earlier I'd seen something in an eastern Turkish market that reminded me of him and had sent him a postcard. Because he worked at Peace Corps/Washington, it was easy for this man of action to get my parents' phone number and learn from my mother where I would be next. By the time I checked for mail at the American Express office in Istanbul, there were three letters waiting. From then on, his letters preceded me across Europe, two or three in every American Express office during the four months I was on the road. In one letter, he observed that *Anastasia* was perhaps too weighty a name to give a baby. What did I think of *Anna*? That should have signaled something, should have prepared me for the phone call months later, for the suggestion of a wedding date.

It did not.

※

On my flight home, I had a one-day layover in D.C. He met me at the airport with a bouquet. I was surprised by the flowers, by how abashed he seemed, surprised that we drove straight from the airport to the Peace Corps office so I could meet his boss. I was jet lagged, shy, introverted, not sure why we were going directly to the nearly empty Peace Corps headquarters on a Saturday afternoon.

Well, I was leaving early the next day, and the man of action wanted to be sure I met his boss, whom he particularly admired. I don't remember what we did the rest of the day. I suppose we walked around, ate dinner, talked, and held hands. I spent the night in his apartment, and he took me to the airport the next morning.

To my surprise, he showed up in Atlanta the following Friday. That evening he had a spirited conversation with my mother who later told me how much she liked him, how smart he was, how interesting. "Eloquent," she said. "Brilliant. Such a good man."

On Saturday, we toured my college campus and stopped in to see a favorite professor, a sweet, soft-spoken woman who was also an alumna of the college. She was a poet and writer who had taken a special interest in me, I hadn't seen her since returning home, and, I suppose, introducing her to him was the equivalent of my meeting his boss in Washington the week before. As we drove away from her house, he commented on the inbred nature of the college, embodied by this professor who arrived as a student and never left. He thought it was funny, quaint, cute, more of a Southern finishing school than academic institution. I was insulted, *deeply* insulted. When he realized how angry I was, he apologized and intimated that he wanted to take care of me, to be my rock, he said. I said I didn't need taking care of, but in 1967, he wasn't the only man who hadn't moved beyond traditional male/female roles where he, *male*, takes care of her, *female*. And to be fair, that was the way his family worked; however, mine did not.

My mother didn't hear that conversation, didn't know how hurt I was when she told me how much she liked him. He was strong, outspoken, opinionated, just the kind of person she liked to spend time with. Well, her judgment meant a lot to me. Perhaps I could overcome his ridiculing my academic background, but I didn't realize the need would arise so quickly.

Here I was, a week later, indirectly agreeing to marry him by choosing a date.

My mother arrived home shortly after the call. I mentioned that he had just phoned and that, apparently, we were getting married on January 20.

Her response was swift and sharp. "Well, I need to see him again before that happens."

And, "How in the hell do you think we can plan a wedding in two months?"

And that night, as my parents and I were eating dinner, my mother said to me, "Don't you have something to tell your father?"

※

I can't explain why I was so timid, so unassertive, so reluctant to speak up and tell my dad I was getting married, or, more importantly, to say to the man himself, "Married? When did we talk about getting married?" I can even admit that it was perhaps my reticence that made him think I was the sort of person who needed taking care of.

Nearly sixty years later we both know each other a lot better: He knows I can take care of myself very well, thank you; I know his natural instinct is to act, to do what he thinks needs to be done and move on. He forges ahead and is on to the next task while I am still considering options. So we frustrate each other, but we know each other, love each other, and want the best for the other. Generosity is the basis of our long marriage.

My mother saw him many times in the years that followed and died knowing her initial assessment was right: he is a good man.

And Anna was born fourteen months after that phone call, although, given more time to consider it, I think we could have named her Anastasia.

Sick in Kisumu

Kisumu was a lonely posting for me. We lived on the edge of a vast, empty plain in the last row of houses on the highway out of town, half a mile south of the equator. A single mango tree grew in the back yard—or was it avocado? I don't remember; it never produced fruit.

Anna was six months old when we arrived in Kisumu, I was pregnant with John, and I had nothing to do. Nothing. Chuck was the Peace Corps representative in western Kenya, primarily for education volunteers, all of whom were a half-day's drive away or more. If he was home, he wasn't working, so he was never home. Never.

Nevertheless, we had two employees. Kezieh had come with us from Nairobi to help with the baby, and Joseph kept us safe at night, every night. We had resisted hiring Joseph, but our landlord insisted: Employing a night watchman was a condition of our rental agreement, especially because Chuck was seldom home.

I liked Joseph. He was a friendly guy and was eager to talk when he arrived each evening at dusk. His most persistent question was "What religion are you?" He asked me that repeatedly; maybe it was the best sentence he could formulate in English. I don't remember just how I prevaricated. Did I dare to say *no religion*? Maybe I said I had been raised Presbyterian. That would have satisfied him, until he probed more deeply: What kind of Presbyterian? What does Presbyterian mean? What does it believe? What do you believe?

By the time we arrived in Kisumu, I had little respect for missionaries and the religion they preached. The missionaries I met in both Ethiopia and Kenya were social conservatives who considered local people their inferiors, savages who needed western salvation and western religion. I wasn't surprised that it was the first question from almost every Kenyan I met, but it made me uncomfortable. "What is your religion?" was meant as a sign of respect and an assumption of piety. I was white, so maybe they assumed I was a missionary and had an answer. I didn't.

Kezieh did have an answer. She was a faithful Seventh Day Adventist. Most Kenyan domestic employees worked six days with Sundays off, but Kezieh needed Saturday free, so she was an exception in that regard. I was to learn she was an exception in other ways. I knew she was Kikuyu, like President Kenyatta, but I don't think either of us realized what life in a Luo stronghold like Kisumu would mean for her until the day the two of us, with Anna on my hip, were at an agricultural fair in the center of town. The word spread quickly that Tom Mboya, a Luo and popular opposition leader, had been murdered that day as he stepped out of a drug store in Nairobi. I couldn't have distinguished physically between a Luo and a Kikuyu, but the local people knew immediately that Kezieh was Kikuyu. The mild interest we'd had in the fair turned to terror as people clustered around us, shouting at Kezieh, "*She is Kikuyu, murderer, murderer like Kenyatta.*"[7]

We ran for the car.

After that, I never let her leave the house alone, so she spent most of her free time isolated in her small room behind our house. I didn't know then she had a child, a boy, Frank, who was a year older than Anna; Frank was being cared for by her extended family so she could work. I imagine she was afraid she would lose her job if we knew she had a child.

Later, much later, she told me of her marriage to a man who left

---

7. Jomo Kenyatta, a Kikuyu, was the first president of Kenya from 1964 to his death in 1978.

her with his family while he went to look for work. Frank was born, her husband never returned, and at some point, she left, escaped, fled, took Frank, and managed to get to a sister who took her in. Her sister worked for somebody we knew and sent Kezieh to us when Chuck was posted to Kisumu. You'll need her, I was told by other staff wives. I didn't want her, not really, but we felt obligated to contribute to the employment of a young woman who needed work and, I learned, I *did* need her. I wasn't up to doing all our laundry by hand in the bathtub: the diapers, the sheets, the towels, my clothes, and Chuck's.

The only people I socialized with, if you could call it that, were the agricultural volunteers, young Peace Corps guys who had been issued motorcycles. They had mobility that other volunteers lacked and took full advantage of it. The trio we called the Sugar Shack guys—Jim, Dennis, and Bob—were my most frequent visitors. I think they stopped by primarily for the free food and, perhaps, a little female conversation. And then there was Jack. Jack was a good looking, personable guy from New Jersey, but vague about his responsibilities, something to do with passion fruit. He did make sure you knew he carried a switch blade.

"Hey, you could hurt somebody with that."

"Only if I mean to," Jack liked to say. "Only if I mean to."

The consensus about Jack was that whatever his posting was, he wasn't clear about what he actually did. He stopped by one day and gave me a ride on the back of the bike—around the block, less than a mile, but memorable because my life was so even then, so uneventful, so without purpose. I had expected to love living in Kenya, but I didn't anticipate the shame of having nothing to do, of living like a kept woman, bound to the house because of the baby, happily connected to her, but with nothing, really nothing meaningful to do.

I did insist on doing my own shopping and always took Anna with me. She was an easy baby, full of smiles, and Kenyans love babies. A wave of excitement rippled through the market when we appeared because here was somebody so new to the world, a baby, a beautiful baby. Her appeal in the local market always earned me an extra tomato or banana—"for the baby," the vendor would say after our contentious bargaining session for the same tomatoes or bananas was finalized. They were right; she was perfect.

She was perfect until the morning I went to get her up, and she lay limp and listless in her crib, her sheets smeared with diarrhea, and her body covered with bright red dots. A mosquito had spent the night *inside* the net I carefully stretched and tucked around her crib every night. The mosquito I had imprisoned her with fed on her all night long. It wouldn't have been a problem in Nairobi, which at 5000 feet is malaria free; Kisumu, on the shores of Lake Victoria, is not.

She was awake, but no smile, no hand grabbing for mine. She didn't roll over, didn't push herself up, didn't stand with arms outstretched, ready to be picked up. When I changed her diaper, her little body seemed half the size of the day before and too pale except for the bites. I scooped her up, tried to feed her, but she refused any food. I dressed her, strapped her in the car seat, and drove to the only doctor I knew of, who operated out of a storefront in town.

It was a bare waiting room, with benches crammed with people around the edges and a Kenyan woman at a table in the middle. I approached her and began explaining what had happened, how sick my baby was, but she wasn't the person to tell. She waved me toward a bench filled with people in the queue ahead of me, all local people, two others with children, the rest adults, nobody I knew. I squeezed between two women on a narrow bench.

I don't remember how I knew to go to this doctor—maybe I'd seen his name on a plaque outside the store front, maybe my next door neighbor, Alwyn, had told me about him. All I really remember is the waiting room, the listless baby in my lap, and the taste of fear in my mouth. Nobody looked at me; nobody wanted to hold Anna, nobody tried to pinch her cheek or offer her a banana. It was a quiet group; nobody spoke or made eye contact. Everybody was sick and nobody expected help soon—the lethargy of people accustomed to waiting.

When the receptionist called a name, the lucky person stood and followed her through a door in the back. The receptionist then resumed her position at the table until that person shuffled out, and the process was repeated. She called the name, escorted the patient back, resumed her post. I had been there an hour or more when the Asian doctor himself appeared at the door. When he saw me, the only *mzungu*, white person, waiting, he said something under his breath to the receptionist, and she called my name next.

"Why did you wait?" His first words, impatient, almost angry. Now, over fifty years later, I wonder at that question. In those days there were three women's restrooms and three men's in every public establishment, each marked by caste: White, Asian, African. The Indians—Asians—in Kenya were caught in the middle during colonial times—and they were still caught five years after independence. The Asian had been made to feel inferior to the European and so went to great lengths to be superior to the African. My presence in this Asian doctor's waiting room called forth an instinctive respect and fear in him. In colonial times, no British woman of any age would allow herself to be placed in a queue to wait; she would demand to be seen immediately if her child were sick. We experienced the same racism, or was it classicism, when John was born unexpectedly early a few months later. "No, no you can't stay here," a British nurse would tell us when we showed up in the middle of the night at a provincial hospital, me in hard labor, John ready to be born. She wouldn't let us stay in that government hospital with black Kenyans, and insisted we go across town to a private hospital. But that's another story.

Anna wasn't the sickest person in that room. Poor people don't show up in a doctor's waiting room with minor complaints; nobody looked well, all were as sick or sicker than my baby.

I don't remember much else about that day. I don't remember what the doctor said was wrong with her; I don't remember what he prescribed. I remember sitting on a hard bench in a barren room with desperately ill people. I remember the weight of an unresponsive child in my arms. I remember the taste of fear in my mouth.

People in American waiting rooms aren't that sick, not like those listless souls who waited until they couldn't hold their heads up to gather a few shillings and trek into town to see Dr. Singh or Dr. Patel. All of them were as sick or sicker than Anna, and she was so sick that I could hardly breathe.

I was glad to be called out of turn, glad the doctor took me next, glad he knew what to do, glad my baby was much better the next day, and relieved when we moved back to Nairobi a few months later where I had friends, a choice of clinics, and nobody yelled at Kezieh because she was Kikuyu.

Safari[8] Surprise

The Naro Moru River Lodge stretches along the river as it cascades off the western slope of Mount Kenya, on its way to the Ewaso Ng'iro River, on to Somalia, and the sea. The lodge facilities were simple in 1970; there was a main building with four guest rooms, a spacious dining room, and a scattering of rustic cottages along the river. The bar closed at 10 p.m., the generator powered off at 11 p.m., and by one-o'clock in the morning, when I woke up again to go to the bathroom, all was dark and quiet.

The drive up from Nairobi that afternoon had been uneventful—not much traffic, a stop at the Outspan Hotel in Nyeri for their famous buffet, then another 42 kilometers to the Naro Moru turnoff, but the last 2 kilometers were washboard road all the way in. I laughed as we bumped along. "I'm glad this isn't the road to the hospital. Just thinking about it could induce labor." I was still a comfortable six weeks from my due date, and we'd made the trip conscious of the impending birth: it would be our last trip out of Nairobi before the baby was born—just an overnight, maybe even a romantic overnight. We'd left thirteen-month old Anna with Kezieh and William the cook at our

---

8. *Safari* is the Swahili word for any journey or trip.

house in Nairobi. They both doted on her, and we'd be back by lunchtime the following day.

I lit the candle in the little bathroom again and wondered why I was there. Second time that night. I didn't really have to pee, but I was up, awake, not feeling quite myself, and not sure what was bothering me. I blew out the candle and stared out the narrow window. Stars above, but no lights in any of the other cottages. The lodge was dark too. I went back to bed, couldn't sleep, thrashed about, got up again, same routine, stand in the bathroom with the candle, blow it out, look out the window, back to the bedroom. The third time I woke Chuck up, told him I couldn't sleep, and admitted I didn't feel right, and crawled in bed with him. We lay there silently for a few more minutes.

At last, I said it. "I think the baby's coming."

"Too early," he said. "Not due."

"I know."

We lay there a while longer, then he said, "Well, we're not getting any sleep. We may as well go to Nyeri." Nyeri was the provincial capital, only 40 kilometers away; there would be a hospital in Nyeri. And if the baby really was coming, we would never make the 175 kilometers back to Nairobi. Labor with Anna thirteen months earlier had been quick; fast for a first baby, the doctor had said.

So we got up, dressed, put our bag in the car, and started it up. Tried to start it. The engine grated but didn't turn over. As Chuck said later, that was when he believed the baby *was* going to be born that night. He dutifully got out of the car, raised the hood as I tried to rev the engine again; nothing. I released the brake, he leaned his shoulder against the trunk and pushed; the car started rolling and then, miraculously, the engine caught, I slid over, he jumped in, and we were bumping over the washboard road we had joked about ten hours earlier.

"We should leave a note," I said.

We hadn't paid for our room or our dinner, but there was no light anywhere, nowhere to leave a note, and once the car was going, we couldn't stop. We were leaving. The road was rough, but when we got to the highway, it was smooth and empty—we never saw another vehicle that night—and the turn off to Nyeri came up after twenty minutes. Chuck slowed to turn, but the road was blocked: "Bridge Out" a sign read.

※

That was when I started mentally reviewing what we should do if the baby came while we were driving, especially if we were on our way to Nairobi. I couldn't think of a thing. My only reassurance was that I had delivered naturally just thirteen months earlier; surely there would be no problem with this birth. Easy peasy.

We kept going and 20 kilometers later there was another turn off to Nyeri. We took it.

In those days Nyeri was a one road town with a string of shops, all dark at two in the morning, but there was a single light at the end of town—the police station. Chuck pulled in, leapt out of the car, and startled the guy on duty. "Hospital?" he yelled, hoping the word was the same in Swahili. "Hospital?" A minute later he came out with a policeman gesturing directions, go here, turn there.

The hospital wasn't far, and there was a light on in one of the buildings near the entrance to the huge compound. We both got out, hurried over, pounded on the door, and startled the nurse on duty—an Englishwoman.

I was so happy to see a fluent English speaker. "My baby is coming," I said. "Now."

She raised her eyebrows. "Well, yes, I see, but you can't stay here."

"Oh, yes, I want to," I said. "Really. Please."

"No, no, no." She had the authoritative voice of somebody used to being obeyed. "You can't stay here. You must go to Mount Kenya hospital. I'll call and tell them you're coming."

I repeated my desire to stay there, with her, to have my baby with her, but she was more sure of herself than I, more adamant, and I realized later that in her opinion a white woman giving birth in a hospital meant for black Kenyans simply wasn't possible. The country had only been independent for a few years; she had probably been born there and, in her mind, colonial norms still ruled. She asserted again that the private hospital was only ten minutes away, and said she would telephone to let them know we were on our way. "Go, go," she said.

She was right about the ten minutes. We found the little hospital easily, but if she had called, nobody heard; the building was completely dark. We knocked on the door, pounded on the door, and finally, saw a light come on at the end of the hallway and a Kenyan nurse walk slowly toward us. She cracked the door, we explained the situation, and she let us in.

"I must have your insurance card," she said.

We had no insurance card, no passport, no documentation, nothing; we explained we were Americans with the embassy, not residents, talking fast until she agreed to let us stay. Then, for some reason, she insisted that I go to the bathroom immediately. I went into hard labor as soon as I sat on the toilet.

She threw open the door when she heard me grunting. "No, no!" she yelled, and pulled me out and onto a bed in an adjacent room and turned on all the lights.

"I am calling the doctor," she said and disappeared.

We heard her in the next room, turning the crank of the telephone until it sprang to life, and she made contact with somebody. She shouted into it, in a combination of Swahili and English, then hung up and returned to us. "The doctor, she is coming."

I was glad a doctor was coming, but knew this young woman could deliver a baby if she had to. I was relieved to be out of the car, in a building with electricity, and with a woman in a nurse's uniform. She stayed with us until the doctor, actually two doctors, arrived: Mrs. Dr. Patel, the obstetrician, and her husband, Mr. Dr. Patel.

The contractions were coming quickly by then. "Wait, wait," Mrs. Dr. Patel said. "I must scrub." She kept up a stream of conversation as she washed. "When are you due?"

"March 15," I said.

"Oh," she said, "Oh! That is *my* due date."

I lifted my head and saw the bulge in her sari—she was as pregnant as I was.

"Who's your obstetrician?"

"Dr. M, in Nairobi," I said.

She laughed. "He is mine too. I better pack my bags."

Noises I couldn't control were coming from me. "Wait, wait," she said again. "I am coming. I will deliver you. Wait, I will deliver you."

I didn't know how to wait when my body was so much in charge. I held on as long as I could, but I couldn't slow down what had started without my permission. The baby was on the way and out as soon as she was there to catch him in her sterilized hands. "A boy," she said, and held him up—small, red, crying, perfect.

The nurse took him. "What will you call him? John?"

"Yes," I admitted, "John." We had decided to name the baby John if he were a boy. Did the young nurse assume all white baby boys were named John? "What time is it?" I said. For some reason it felt important to know what time he was born.

"5:15."

"John," I said. "John born at 5:15 am in Nyeri, Kenya, weighing 5 pounds 3 ounces." Chuck was in the room by then, receiving congratulations, both of us happy, pleased, and greatly relieved.

The Patels whispered together, then asked Chuck to step out of the room for a minute. The placenta hadn't come down, and they were afraid I would go into shock if I were conscious when Dr. Patel removed it. They needed an anesthesiologist, but the only one in town didn't have a phone. Mr. Dr. Patel would drive to the anesthesiologist's house, wake him up, and bring him back to the hospital. Did Chuck approve this extra step?

Yes.

I don't remember how long it was before the Kenyan anesthesiologist arrived with the good Mr. Dr. Patel, put me under, Mrs. Dr. Patel successfully removed the placenta, and I slept on.

The three doctors washed up and went home, the nurse was ready to go back to bed, and, suddenly, Chuck had nothing to do and nowhere to go. He stood around for a bit, then got back in the car and drove over to the Outspan Hotel, where we had had lunch the previous afternoon. A man at the bar was starting coffee, and obviously surprised to see a white man appear just as the sun came up.

"I need a room and a drink. Cognac."

The bartender paused, looking as if he hadn't understood.

"My son was just born."

"Ah, Bwana, that is good," the man said. "What did you name him?"

"John."

"And what is your father's name?"

"John."

"Ah, *mzuri sana, Bwana*. Very good, Sir." The bartender poured the brandy. The new father had done it just right, named his first son after his own father. Very good. *Mzuri sana*.

Amazing.

Our Beautiful Boy

They sent us his picture: Alejandro, six years old and waiting. His mother had signed the papers giving him up a few months earlier, but the nuns in Bucaramanga didn't bring him to Bogota until after she died. I have often thought of his mother, wondered about her story, wondered how she could say goodbye to her beautiful child, and am not surprised that she waited as long as she could, waited until she knew she wouldn't be there to love him and to raise him. She couldn't leave him until she knew he would be taken care of.

So he wasn't abandoned; he was protected and planned for. We know she loved him because she figured out how to keep him safe. We also know she loved him because from the very beginning, he was a healthy boy, a sweet boy, a boy who showed none of the trauma we had heard was evident in other children adopted at his age: no cigarette burns on his body, no fear of adults, no uncontrollable wailing. He was sad when he realized what had happened to him, but he had been loved and protected, and it was easy for us to love him and keep him safe.

We arrived in Bogota on a Sunday and found a cheap hotel on a busy corner not far from the center of the city. It was an intersection with no stop signs or stop lights, so cars, trucks, and taxis leaned on their horns to announce their presence throughout the night. It didn't matter; we wouldn't have slept much that night anyway. Our appointment at FANA, *Fundación para la Asistencia de la Niñez Abandonada*, Foundation for the Assistance of Abandoned Children, was first thing the next morning, March 7, 1977.

FANA was in an attractive, one-story building in a well-kept Bogota neighborhood. The receptionist greeted us, took our names, and indicated that we should sit on the two chairs across from her desk. Our Spanish was as limited as her English, and so we expected she would return with a social worker or with the founder and director, Mercedes (Rosario Pineda de Martinez), with whom we'd been communicating. We were looking forward to meeting Mercedes, to learning more about Alejandro, and what was required of us before we could take him home.

The receptionist returned almost immediately with a handsome, quiet boy by the hand. "He is here," she said, and returned to her desk.

He was as startled as we were at his sudden presentation to two adults he had never seen before and, as would become evident, with whom he shared no common language. I am not clear on what happened next. I know we had brought pictures of Anna and John, of our dog Dixie, of our house and the neighborhood; we showed him the pictures, identified the people, the buildings, the existence of snow. He looked at it all politely, and I am guessing was at a loss as to what to think or even to know what he was looking at or why. None of us knew what was supposed to happen next.

After twenty minutes or so, I approached the receptionist. "What are we supposed to do now? Are there papers?"

She seemed surprised by the question and indicated that we could take him with us but should have him back by sundown.

Really?

At some point, somebody must have given us papers to sign; somebody must have explained that we had to get him a passport and a visa to enter the United States, but I don't remember who or how or when. We did visit the sprawling American embassy later that week, took him for a required medical checkup, received a sheaf of papers that we signed, stamped, and paid for. There must have been considerable paperwork both at FANA and at the Embassy, but what I remember, what stands out are the days we spent exploring Bogota with our beautiful boy.

That first day we took a taxi from FANA back to the center of Bogota and walked and walked and walked. At lunchtime, we went into a small restaurant. We couldn't read the menu, but as far as we could tell, the waiter offered Alex some choices. He told the man what he wanted and so I ordered the same thing. It was liver. I don't eat liver, don't like liver, but I nibbled around the edges and did my best to pretend it was wonderful, while he cleaned his plate.

That afternoon we stopped at the toy department in a large store and invited him to choose whatever he wanted. That was clearly a foreign idea to him, an option he'd never had and couldn't comprehend. We eventually realized he had no experience with that kind of choice and bought something simple and universal: a ball. He was delighted. We also had him try on pants and a shirt and a blue jumpsuit. He liked the jumpsuit best, so we bought that too. Later, we would buy *ruanas* for him and for Anna and John, and a few Colombian artifacts, but what struck me was how surprised he was to receive gifts; pleased, but surprised. He only asked for one thing that week: to have his shoes polished. Neither Chuck nor I had ever had shoes polished by a shoeshine man, but Alex knew what was required to be properly dressed in his new clothes, and so his shoes were buffed to a radiant shine.

We had a few necessary appointments, like the trip to the Embassy and the doctor, but we spent most of our time seeing the sights of Bogota: souvenir shops, the gold museum, and The Salt Cathedral of Zipaquirá, an underground Roman Catholic church built in the tunnels of a salt mine about 30 miles from Bogota. We had planned to take a local bus and managed to find the bus station and even where to stand to get the right bus to Zipaquirá. But, as we were waiting in that sprawling bus park teaming with people, a policeman approached us, and through a series of gestures, pointing at Chuck's camera, my purse, and swiping his forefinger across his throat, indicated that we wouldn't be safe on a bus, any bus. Oh. Okay. We took a taxi to the Salt Cathedral.

Two other moments stand out from that week.

The large playroom at FANA was just past the hallway of offices beyond the reception area. When we arrived for Alex the second morning, we could see him at the end of the hallway; not playing with the other children, not even watching them, but sitting on a bench, waiting for us. He looked anxious, perhaps not sure we would come, but he was waiting and, I like to think, he was *hoping* we would come. We were already in love, already completely sure that he was our son, and the sight of him waiting for us made it mutual. He wanted us too.

The next moment broke our hearts. The three of us were walking in a large park when suddenly Chuck said, "Cross the street and keep walking." He said it twice, insistently. I didn't know what the problem was but took Alex's hand and crossed the street.

I looked back in time to see a man sitting on the curb of the sidewalk with a child in his lap, a beautiful little girl, two or three years old. The man was cradling his dead child, rocking back and forth and weeping. Chuck slipped some pesos in his lap, and we walked on. I don't think Alex saw. But writing this now, I realize he may have seen more of the loss and tragedy of poverty in his short life than I had, but neither of us wanted him to see that.

He was obviously a healthy, well-coordinated child, but we thought we would learn more of his story, of his past life, of what was known about him. Now more than fifty years later I wish we had asked more questions . . . and maybe we did . . . but what I have written here is all that we know. Language was an issue, and we were only there a week. By the following Saturday we were on the plane home. My parents met us at the airport; Chuck's mother was waiting at our house with Anna and John and the new pajamas she had made for all three of them. We took pictures of our three children and knew we were blessed.

And still are.

The Lucky Family

Chuck was interviewing for a wide variety of positions, including focusing on both of our home states, Georgia and Minnesota (to be near our extended families) and I wanted to be ready to go anywhere. So ending up in Minnesota was fortunate, because his father had died two months before we arrived and his mother was still recovering from the loss. She needed us, Chuck needed to be there, and we were glad to be close. We found a beautiful four-bedroom house on a quiet street not far from where he had grown up. It was perfect.

Except.

Except I felt at loose ends, not connected, and I will admit, shocked to be in the most homogeneous city I had ever lived in. So I was delighted that first summer when I saw a one paragraph article in the local paper that said the International Center at the University of Minnesota was looking for families to host exchange students for three weeks as part of the university's orientation program for international students. Yes, we could do that!

I could have called, but I was too shy to pick up the phone, so I drove over there, found somebody in the office, and explained that we were interested in hosting an international student, from Africa, if possible. A few days later, they let us know that we would be welcoming a young man in late August, Gladstone M. from South Africa.

They gave us his home address, so I wrote him, told him how happy we were that that he would be spending his orientation weeks with us, introduced our little family, and readied a bedroom for him. It never occurred to me to mention that we were white, even though South Africa was ruled by the apartheid government at that time.

It clearly never occurred to him that we wouldn't be black. He never said as much, but he was *so* surprised, so very uncomfortable, that he hardly spoke for the first two days. Our responsibility was to welcome him as a member of the family, to be sure he knew how to take the bus from our house to the U of M every day for his orientation programs, and, in general, introduce him to life in these United States. It took him days to relax around us, but as we got to know him, (and he us), we saw how blessed we were to have such a smart, gentle, interested, and interesting man in our lives. He was most comfortable around the children, but also became comfortable with Chuck and me as time went on.

Gladstone was such a welcome gift to us, that we signed up to host an international student for several years after and were delighted and enriched by the young men—always men, for some reason—from Cameroon, Egypt, Iran, Nigeria, and Morocco whom we hosted for the summer orientation, then invited for holidays and other events in the year that followed. It was good for us all, and a wonderful introduction to people from around the world for Anna, John, and Alex.

❋

We were on our way to a Sunday afternoon family event at Chuck's cousin's house when the phone rang. It was Judy, a neighbor who lived behind us, across the alley. We knew each other well enough to wave and smile but had never really spoken. She introduced herself, reminded me which house she lived in, and explained that as a Social Worker with Lutheran Social Services, she was involved in the

Unaccompanied Minors program created after the end of the Viet Nam war for children separated from their families. Her family often hosted a young person in their home until a permanent placement was found for that boy or girl.

She was calling because they had a sixteen-year-old boy from Ethiopia, Ahmed, the first Ethiopian to arrive in Minnesota under the Unaccompanied Minors Program, who was living with them until his permanent placement could be determined. Lutheran Social Services *had* found a place for him, Judy said, and named the location, a Minneapolis suburb with very few people of color. "He is *such* a nice guy," she said. "I am just not comfortable sending him there." A neighbor had told her that we had spent time in Ethiopia . . . were we interested?

"We are just now heading out the door for a family event," I said. "I'll call you back as soon as we are home again."

*

On the way to the party I told Chuck and the kids about the phone call and the possible addition to the family. Our three teenagers would be the only young people at the event, and we knew they would probably spend most of their time in the basement playing pool in the cousin's rec room, which they did.

As soon as we were back in the car on the way home, all three of them, thirteen, fourteen, and fifteen years old at the time, said, "Yep, let's invite him to live with us."

I called Judy. "Yes, we'd love to have him as part of our family," I said.

"Don't you want to meet him first?"

Well, it didn't seem right to interview a young guy who had been separated from his family for who knows how long and undergone trauma and struggles we knew nothing about . . . but Judy insisted. Ahmed came over the next evening to meet us. He was, as she said, a wonderful young man, and we knew from the very beginning that he was, and is, the nicest guy, thoughtful and considerate, and just right to be the oldest kid in our family. We were so lucky.

※

Judy called again a year later. Her family was about to leave on a road trip, but a young guy from Eritrea, Jamal, had just arrived and was staying with them as he waited for a permanent placement. It didn't feel right for them to take him on a long car trip so soon after his arrival. Could he stay with us for a week, without the expectation that it would be a permanent placement? Just five days, maybe seven.

Of course.

Before those seven days were up, each of our kids, Ahmed, Anna, John, and Alex came to Chuck or me individually and said, "Can we keep him?"

And so we did. Our family was complete and, I must say, brag in fact, our family was quite wonderful, even amazing.

Back row, Ahmed and Alex; Front row, Anna, John, Jamal.

Proxy

Mohammed Aduss and I had never seen each other—not even in photographs—but he grabbed both my shoulders and kissed me hard on the mouth when we met. I was not his son, but his son, Ahmed, was safe in my house in Minneapolis, so he kissed me as if I were the lost boy himself.

We could hardly speak after that first kiss. I looked away in embarrassment, and he kissed me again.

I've seen pictures of a lost child reunited with his family. There's a bewildered joy in those faces, an emotion as overwhelming as death. We aren't prepared for that fierce joy beyond happiness and laughter. Perhaps the human psyche wasn't constructed to sustain the shock of reunion, just as we're not meant to be forever separated from our children. Ahmed was twelve years old the last time his father had seen him. He was twenty-three when I met his father in Ethiopia.

His father's face pulsed with emotion. Ahmed shows nothing in his face. He covers his mouth when he laughs and turns away when he is sad. He had given me a cousin's phone number in Addis Ababa, but he didn't tell me anything about the rest of the family. I knew two of his cousins' names, Anisa and Ekram, but not the names of his parents or brothers or sisters; neither of us thought I'd see them.

I'd arrived in Ethiopia on a Saturday, stayed with friends, and we'd called the cousin, Anisa, on Monday morning and arranged to meet her at my friend Innes' office at the University. Innes and I were waiting on the steps when an old car with three people in it pulled up. The driver was a plump, mature woman swathed in the traditional scarves and skirts—Anisa. A man in a khaki sports coat and white skull cap sat next to her and a younger woman in jeans and a denim jacket was in the back seat. The car stopped; they got out.

I stepped forward and introduced myself.

"I am Ekram," the young woman in jeans said in English, "and this is Mohammed Aduss."

I put my hand out, but he grabbed me by the shoulders and kissed me. I realized immediately that he was Ahmed's father—the name was right, and he had his son's angular build. My instinct was to embrace him, but he was in charge, and all his emotion was in those kisses.

We stood there laughing and crying. Nobody knew what to say. Finally, Innes herded us into her office and sent out for coffee.

"Mohammed Aduss has been looking for you," Ekram said. "He went to every hotel and to the airport."

"I am so sorry," I said. "Tell him that I'm sorry. I had no idea he knew I was coming."

When Ekram conveyed my apology, Mohammed leapt up and kissed me again. Every vein in his sharp face was visible. The room could not contain his emotion. At first, I thought he was simply glad that Ahmed had found a good home with us, but it was more than that. I was living proof that Ahmed was alive and well. Mohammed didn't kiss me because I had been Ahmed's guardian for the past five years; he kissed me as if I were Ahmed himself, his son in the flesh.

When the coffee came, we clutched the cups gratefully, glad to have somewhere to put our hands, but too nervous to drink. I was so rattled that several minutes passed before I remembered to take out the pictures I'd brought of Ahmed. Mohammed stared at the snapshots of the son he hadn't seen in eleven years and then at me, back and forth. Anisa and Ekram giggled over Ahmed's long hair.

I don't know what I expected from this meeting. Until that morning, I hadn't known it would happen. Harar, where Ahmed's family lives, is over 500 kilometers from Addis Ababa. I didn't expect to go to Harar; I didn't expect his father to come to Addis. I was in Ethiopia to gather material for a novel, and had some notion that Ahmed's cousins would have me over for dinner, to meet the branch of the family that lived in Addis Ababa, and that I might see them two or three more times before I left Ethiopia. It hadn't occurred to me that I would move in with the extended family for the duration of my time in Ethiopia, that I wouldn't be free to do *anything* else. It hadn't occurred to them that any other arrangement was possible. They invited me to lunch that afternoon. I told Innes I'd see her later, got in Anisa's car, and disappeared for two weeks. They kidnapped me.

*

Eleven years earlier, in 1978, Ahmed, with his two older brothers, attended a demonstration of students in Harar. The students were congregated on the main square when the soldiers appeared. Ahmed is hazy on the sequence of events or even why they were there—he just went with his brothers. His oldest brother was killed outright, the next, Abdulnasser, thrown in jail, and Ahmed ran and hid. Three days later, Abdulnasser was released from jail. He found Ahmed, but they were afraid to go home.

It took them thirty-three days to cross the desert to Djibouti, hiding during the day, walking at night with others fleeing the cruel dictatorship of Mengistu Haile Mariam. The period in which Ahmed fled came to be known as the Red Terror. Every family lost somebody; every family wore black for years.

Ahmed and his brother lived hand to mouth for six months in Djibouti, on the Red Sea, where the hottest temperatures on earth are recorded, until the U.N. declared them official refugees and took them to Egypt. Ahmed spent four years in Alexandria, went to school there, before he came to Minnesota.[9] His brother was in Atlanta. They never saw their family in those four years. When I think of Ahmed's story, I imagine my other three children, Anna, John, and Alex, going downtown for some rally and never coming home again.

※

I spent five days at his cousin Anisa's house. On the second day, I realized that Mohammed had come to Addis Ababa for the sole purpose of taking me home to Harar to meet the rest of the family. I didn't think it was possible. All internal travel by nonresidents had to be approved by the Ethiopian Tourist Organization, and I had already been refused permission to go to Dilla where I had taught as a Peace Corps Volunteer. We went to the E.T.O. anyway and learned that since Harar is one of the historical cities in Ethiopia, I could go on the approved government tour and stay at the government hotel for one day only. That wasn't what Mohammed had in mind.

"Is there no other way?"

"Only if you are visiting a relative," the clerk said.

I looked at Mohammed Aduss. "I am visiting a relative," I said. "Give me the form."

When I got to the blank asking for my relationship to the person I was visiting, I wrote, "my son's father," and gave Mohammed's house and *kebele* number. The clerk read over my application without comment, asked for $15 in American currency, and told me to return in three days.

It was four days before I got back to the E.T.O. office because nobody in Anisa's household had a sense of urgency and Harari etiquette wouldn't allow them to let me leave the compound alone, much less

---

9. A sponsor was found for Abdul Nasser first, but he refused to leave Ahmed in Egypt until a sponsor organization was found for Ahmed.

go across town to pick up my travel documents. I pointed out that I was forty-five years old, that I had lived in Ethiopia for two years previously, that I spoke Amharic, that I knew my way around Addis and, in fact, had walked all over the city, alone, for two days before I called them, but if I opened the compound gate, they ran after me: "What do you want? Where are you going?"

I quickly learned that if I told them where I was going, they would go for me or, in the case of the travel papers, reassure me by saying, "Don't worry, we will get them."

One morning, I tried to go to the post office to mail some letters. "Okay, Sammy will go for you." Sammy was Anisa's teenage son.

"Okay, but I also want to buy some aerograms."

"He will buy for you."

"Thank you," I said. "Here is the money." But Anisa wouldn't let me pay for my own aerograms. I put the money on a table, Anisa threw it back; I left it there and walked away; she grabbed my purse and put the money in it. This happened every time I needed something; I couldn't bear to have them pay for my film, my aspirin, my postcards, and they couldn't bear the sight of my money.

I particularly wanted to take the bus to Harar, especially since I'd been refused permission to travel anywhere else. I was eager to travel overland to soak up as much of the Ethiopian countryside as possible before I had to leave. I tried to explain this to Mohammed Aduss, but he closed his face to me. No, the bus was too rough for me.

I knew flying was expensive. "How much is it?"

He wouldn't tell me. Finally, I relinquished all desire for souvenirs or toiletries, and stifled my need to pay my own way—I was in Ethiopia for three weeks and probably didn't spend $50.

*

At home, Ahmed is the first person to clear the table after dinner; he *notices* when the garbage bag is full and takes it out without being asked. He remembers everybody's birthday; he is solicitous of his new relatives, particularly his grandparents. It was clear from his first week as a member of our family that he had been raised by people with definite expectations of correct behavior.

I told him once that he was a perfect son, and he didn't deny it, but his manner was self-effacing. Our only conflicts were when I asked him to do something that clearly violated his sense of propriety.

"Ahmed, look at me when you're speaking," I'd say. "I can't tell what you want."

He'd turn his face toward mine, but the eyes wouldn't follow. He'd cover the side of his face with his long hand. "I can't, Mom."

I knew that he really couldn't look straight at me when making a request, that it was against his cultural norm for child to parent, but it was frustrating that it took so long to figure out what he wanted—especially when I wanted to give him whatever it was. Ahmed is one of those people who are so generous and selfless that my natural instinct was to give him more than he asked for—because he seldom asked.

*

The more I tried to tell Mohammed Aduss exactly what I needed or wanted to do, the easier it was for him to refuse me. "I really want to ride the bus to Harar," I said, looking him straight in the eye.

Impossible.

*

Mohammed and I finally left for Harar on Friday. We kissed Anisa goodbye at the entrance to the airport, showed our tickets to a soldier at the door and were passed along a phalanx of taciturn, armed men who funneled us into the main departure terminal.

We were without translators for the first time. My Amharic had reappeared rapidly during my immersion into the family, but I was slow to realize that Mohammed didn't speak Amharic much better than I did, even though it was the national language. He was fluent in Oromo and Arabic in addition to his mother tongue, Aderage, but not Amharic. It was also our first extended period alone together, and we each fell into one of the predictable strategies for communicating with a person with whom you don't share a common tongue. I began speaking loudly, slowly, and distinctly, as if my increased volume would overcome my inability to speak Aderage. Mohammed, on the other hand, pressed his lips together and gestured at me silently and imperiously, as if I were incapable of interpreting any sound at all.

The din and confusion in the terminal were overwhelming. Dozens of people pressed toward uniformed airline agents behind a long counter. The numbers one through eight were posted at regular intervals high above the counter, but there was no sign in any language to indicate which agent we should approach. Neither of us knew how to proceed, so I collared a man in an official-looking uniform and asked him which counter was for the flight to Dire Dawa. Number seven.

"*Sabat!*" I shouted at Mohammed Aduss, pointing at the number seven swinging over a counter some distance away. "*Sabat!*" There were maybe thirty-five people huddled around the agent at number seven. "Let's get in line there," I yelled slowly, for some reason imagining that an orderly queue would work.

He pressed his lips together, grabbed my arm and pulled me to the front of the crowd at number seven. I pulled back, embarrassed at breaking in line, but he slapped our tickets on the counter and the agent took them in spite of the thirty people ahead of us, tagged our bags, stamped our tickets, gave us the appropriate coupons, gave the bags back to us, and sent us to the gate. None of the people Mohammed had dragged me past protested; neither did the agent.

Our tickets were scrutinized by another armed soldier—this happened seven times in all—then we queued up to go through the metal detector, with ten people ahead of us. Mohammed again tried to push to the front. Because I was still under the illusion that I knew more about airport etiquette than he did, I tried to take control of the situation. "No," I explained loudly, "there is no hurry. Let's just get in line like everybody else." I even allowed a portly man to take his time to pass through ahead of me. Mohammed gestured at me furiously over the fat man's head, but I went through on my own. When we got to the gate, Mohammed motioned to me to sit down. I did. He paced in front of the cloudy window for a bit, then sat on the edge of the seat across from me with his elbows on his knees and his hands clasped before him, staring out the window where the plane would appear.

"Well, we made it," I said. "It's fine."

The sound of my voice startled him. With a clenched smile he acknowledged my ability to speak and lit a cigarette. He was ready to be in Harar.

※

I'd traveled to every province in Ethiopia when I was a Peace Corps Volunteer and had been to Dire Dawa where our plane would land that day, but I'd not gone the extra hundred kilometers to Harar on the eastern ridge of the Great Rift Valley. I was excited to be going at last. Harar is a famous, walled city that has been a center of trade and Islamic learning in the Horn of Africa since the seventh or eighth century. Great Harari caravans carried fruits, vegetables, coffee, saffron, *khat*, and slaves to the provinces of Ethiopia and to the Red Sea coast, and the city is still known for the ninety-nine mosques within the walls, ornate basketwork, and fine silversmithing.

When explorer Richard Burton approached Harar in 1854, he was warned that he would be killed if it were discovered that he was an infidel, but he entered one of the five gates without incident and described the city as poor, infested with smallpox and characterized by "lax moral habits." Shortly after Burton's departure, the Emir of Harar decreed that all women should clothe their legs in the tight-fitting velvet pants that Harari women, including Ahmed's sisters, still wear under their voluminous slips and skirts.

The French poet Arthur Rimbaud entered Harar twenty years later, unaware that Burton had preceded him. Rimbaud fancied himself a

"Northern barbarian" and was confident that *he* would be the first European the Hararis had seen, but when the gates swung open at dawn, Rimbaud was greeted by a blue-eyed Capuchin priest whose first words were, *"Vous parlez francais?"*

Burton and Rimbaud arrived on foot with camels. Mohammed Aduss and I arrived from Dire Dawa in a low-slung Peugeot station wagon cum taxi that deposited us at the bus park outside the walls. Mohammed grabbed my bag, and we entered Harar on foot through the western gate. His posture changed as we entered the city. He walked with his toes pointed out, each foot flying forward before it touched the ground, claiming every inch of earth, nodding to bystanders who called his name. He was not entirely oblivious of me stumbling behind, but he was clearly ready to be home.

I stumbled on the rough road because I was staring at everybody staring at me. "*Ferengi!*" somebody called. It pleased me to be called *ferengi* after so many years. I waved, but Mohammed shouted something at the boy who called to me and sped up. Just before we made the sharp turn down the narrow path that led to his compound, an old man stepped in front of me. "Cuba!" he said.

It took me a minute to understand what he said, then I remembered that the Cubans and the Russians had occupied Ethiopia ever since the United States left after Emperor Haile Selassie was deposed. "No," I said. "American."

"Ah! *Vive* American!" he said and grabbed for my hand. In the days that followed, people grew misty-eyed when they learned I was an American and asked if I knew Mr. Bob who taught them in the Peace Corps, or Mrs. Susan. The conceit of Rimbaud was seductive. It was easy for me to imagine that I was special there, the first American who had been to Harar in fifteen years. The Hararis greeted me with the nostalgia of a people who had suffered under the hands of the foreigners who succeeded us. By the time I got back to Addis Ababa a week later, I had begun to believe in American benevolence until I spoke with a man who was inspecting the box I was sending home. "Oh, you are American? Yes, well, this office was the office of the American

Mapping Mission." He shrugged. "Now it belongs to the Russians. It is the same thing. We do our work on your desks."

✱

Mohammed shouted something, and I ran to catch up. We hurried through the central square, down a rock road, past the mosque where Mohammed worships, and up a sharp right into a narrow, rock path between two eight-foot walls. Without warning he stepped through an arched gate, and we were in a compound filled with people who were grinning at me. Mohammed appeared to make a hasty introduction, then issued a string of orders. He had delivered me safely and now was impatient with the drama of the moment.

I was trying to discern which woman was Ahmed's mother, and I approached the wrong person. That woman covered her face with her hand to hide her laughter—just as Ahmed does—but shook her head furiously. They all laughed and pushed Mama forward. She was a short, shy woman with long hair braided in buns around her ears and covered with a scarf. She kissed me on the cheek, one, two, three times. We stepped back to look at each other. She was smiling broadly, and I was wiping tears from my eyes. She'd been waiting for me, Ahmed's stand-in, for a long time. She didn't try to speak, and I was incoherent. "I am so happy to be here," I repeated several times. It was all I could think of to say.

Hamza, a cousin, spoke English and began telling me who everybody was, but I couldn't absorb it all. I met Ahmed's sisters: Shukuria, who had a new baby, Asiah, Badria, Amira, Maria, Sa'ada. They kissed me shyly. Ahmed's two younger brothers, Abdusalem and Abdukadir, were even stiffer. I learned their names later; at the time, I didn't know whom I was kissing and crying over.

We were standing in the courtyard. Three other houses opened on to the same courtyard, and people were crowded at all the doors to gawk. There were chickens in the yard and several cats. A raggedy girl, who I later realized was a servant, was filling a pot with water at a spigot in the center of the courtyard. Suddenly, Mohammed Aduss said something, and everybody was quiet. Mama hurried a couple of the girls to the kitchen on the opposite side of the compound, the boys faded back to the wall, Hamza grabbed my bag, and he and Mohammed escorted me into the house.

The house was a traditional Harari house. One wall of the central room was completely open to the courtyard; there were five levels to that room, not as stair steps, but in L's and U's that differed in elevation by 10 or 12 inches. Traditionally, only men sat on the highest level, women the next, boys on the right, girls on the left, and the lowest, common area was in the middle. Each level was layered with carpets and the walls were adorned with baskets, quotations from the Koran, and various niches that were originally sized to hold specific oils and holy books.

Up a narrow staircase was the room where I would sleep in a big double bed—Ahmed's parents' room, I assumed; there was a second room at the same level that the girls shared. This room contained a double bed and walls covered with forty brightly painted trays and plates that were startlingly wonderful to look at. Below the girls' room, with a door that opened onto the courtyard, was the boys' room. Ahmed's sister Shukuria and her new baby slept in an alcove off the ground floor. Normally she lived in Addis with her husband and nine-year-old son, but she was spending several months in Harar with her mother during her confinement. All the girls and women worked continuously while I was there, except for Shukuria. Her sole responsibility was to take care of her new son.

The furnishings of the common area consisted of embroidered pillows and a television set that they turned on each evening, thinking I wanted it. The programs were in English, and none of them ever glanced at it.

They had been cooking for days before my arrival. They seated me on the floor on the upper level of the main room and brought on the food: a large plate of plain pasta; chicken stew with hard boiled eggs; a plate of tomatoes; a plate of *injera*; boiled meat and potatoes; potato chips; another plate of cold tomatoes, carrots, potatoes, and beets; boiled greens; fried chicken; fried hamburger; cabbage and potatoes; bananas; a huge platter of white rice with raisins. Mama set the rice in front of me, and all the raisins flew off.

I was handed a warm Coca-Cola and told to eat. Everybody was watching me. I took a piece of bread, and they all grinned.

※

At our round table at home, I sit next to Ahmed and each night I see him carefully remove the potato peelings or the tomato skin or the apple peeling and hold these inedible parts in his left hand below the table. He is so thin that I am always after him to eat, eat, eat. "There are a lot of nutrients in the skins of things," I tell him.

"Yes, Mom," he says, but he continues to conceal the peelings beneath the table. He has trouble with other food. I cook only brown rice because the whole grain is more nutritious and has a fuller flavor, but, after six weeks in our house, Ahmed pointed to the rice on our table. "This has no taste. You should try white rice."

※

I ate as much as I could, but my stomach was churning.

"*Bie, bie.* Eat, eat," Mohammed Aduss urged every time I paused. He filled my bowl full of food I couldn't possibly get down and waved his finger at me whenever I faltered. "Eat! Eat!"

Every meal progressed like that, with Mohammed shouting, "Eat! Eat!" and me eating as much as I could to please him. Between meals they paraded me around to neighbors and relatives who fed me again. By the evening of the second day, I had a migraine. Ahmed's mother brought me fried ground meat swimming in grease and a bowl of canned pineapple for supper. It appeared that I was the only person who was going to eat. "No, I can't," I said. "You eat, please."

They were desperate for me to eat. Mohammed, Mama, the three sisters who lived at home all entreated me to eat. "Please," Amira said. So I tasted the meat and swallowed a chunk of pineapple. The pineapple tasted like aluminum. "Excuse me," I said and rushed past them, across the courtyard, and into the outhouse where I was repeatedly sick to my stomach. They could all hear me.

When I came back, the food was out of sight. "I am sorry," I said. Maria insisted on washing my feet; Sa'ada stood with me as I brushed my teeth in the courtyard, then the three girls took me up to bed and left me alone. I pulled the sheet up over my head and cried, ashamed to be sick and unable to eat what they gave me and thinking of Ahmed with the potato skins in his left hand under the table.

※

After we ate that first day, we lounged on the carpets for the coffee ceremony. The oldest sister Asiah roasted the green coffee beans over a charcoal fire, then ground them with a mortar and pestle as we watched, then made the coffee in a clay pot over the charcoal fire. The men smoked cigarettes or chewed *khat*. Incense burned in the corner of the room as we waited for the coffee. My lungs were filled with the smoke and incense in the unventilated space—I wondered how they could breathe—but nobody commented on the density of the air.

"This is how we relax," Asiah's husband, Abebekar, said when coffee was served. "All the family taking coffee together, talking, praying. Do you do this in America?"

I sipped the rich black coffee and admitted that we didn't.

When the coffee was finished, I got out the pictures of Ahmed to show his mother. Mohammed hadn't let me show them when I first arrived. He'd wagged his finger at me when I pulled the small albums out of my bag as they were bringing the food and spoke his first word to me since we'd left Anisa in Addis. "No."

Ahmed's sisters were impressed with the pictures, particularly with Ahmed's long hair. "He is so old," Amira said.

I nodded. "Americans say he looks like Michael Jackson."

His mother looked at each picture for a long time before turning to the next. When I told her the photo books were hers to keep, she grinned and nodded. She had prominent, white teeth that made her smile memorable. When I think of her now, I see that radiant smile and her short body bent to some task. The only times I saw her not working were when she was praying or looking at the pictures.

I expected to be left with the women in Harar as I had been in Addis, but Mohammed controlled my schedule there. In Addis, he'd been subdued. At home in Harar, he was imperious and impatient, the center of everything. I was never alone with Mama or the girls. Mama and I never really spoke—she was too shy and too busy. If I tried to help her, Mohammed dragged me away. If one of the girls sidled up to talk or sit with me, he ordered them to do some task. I was his responsibility.

When things got too awkward, I wrote in my notebook. Mohammed was relieved to have me occupied and smoked and talked to the men who came by. Every time I looked up, somebody was staring at me. Khalid, Mohammed's grandson, sat very close to me, whispering and staring the whole time, reporting my every movement to the others.

They prayed without embarrassment in front of everyone, including me, while the others kept on talking. Asiah wrapped her feet in a scarf, (her head and hands were already covered), and stood as she began praying. I was clearly in the way, but I didn't know where to move to. I was sitting where they put me, on the floor with three pillows behind my back—the only person with pillows. Asiah finished and Mohammed began his prayers with little Khalid. They prayed, kneeled, touched their head to the rug, stood up, and continued praying. Nobody seemed to mind that I was there writing. In fact, a couple of days later, when the girls were praying, they asked me to take their picture. "No, I can't," I said. "It isn't right."

"Yes, please. Show them how we pray in America."

※

There are ninety-nine mosques within the walls of tiny Harar. There were two in Minneapolis at that time. The one at the University of Minnesota met at 1:30 p.m. on Fridays—Ahmed was in school on Fridays—so on a Saturday I drove him to the Islamic Center of Minnesota. We passed several large churches as we looked for the address. "That must be it," Ahmed said, indicating a particularly impressive church.

"No, I don't think so," I said. A few minutes later we found the Islamic Center in a small frame house.

"This is the wrong place," Ahmed said.

"It's the right address," I said. "I'll wait for you while you check it out."

An hour later, he came out, subdued. "How was it?" I asked.

He shrugged. "It was good."

"Were there other Ethiopians?"

"No, they were Pakistanis and Indians."

He never went back.

※

Everybody in Harar asked if Ahmed was praying. "It is hard," I said, but my inability to explain why it is hard for him to pray went beyond the language limitations.

In Harar, the voices of the muezzins in the mosques fill the air five times a day. The early morning streets are crowded with men in white robes returning from the mosque. Asiah and Abebekar go to Arabic lessons from 6:00 am to 7:30 am every morning. Ahmed's mother prays as his father carries on a lively conversation, even interrupting her from time to time. She answers his questions and goes back to her prayers.

We took Ahmed to our Unitarian Universalist Church, to the youth group with our other children. He went and had friends there. We didn't hear the call of the muezzin in Minneapolis. And none of us prayed.

※

I was in Harar because Ahmed couldn't be—it was still too dangerous for him to go. While I was there, it occurred to me that if Ahmed became an American citizen, he could travel to Ethiopia as I had, on an American passport. I had met an Ethiopian refugee in Addis Ababa who had done just that. Ahmed was desperate to go home. His parents were in their sixties, and he was afraid that they would die before he saw them again. I told Mohammed that Ahmed wanted to come home.

"No," Mohammed said, "he must finish school first." (Ahmed was in his second year of college then.)

"But it would mean so much to him. He wants to see you and his mother and sisters and brothers. Then he can finish."

"Yes, he will finish. Then he will come," Mohammed said.

We had this conversation without a translator, and I struggled for the words to explain the hole in Ahmed's heart, to explain how much he needed to see that everybody was all right before he could get on with his life. Ahmed had received his first pictures from his family the second spring he was with us. It was the only time I'd seen him break down. He held the picture of Sa'ada, his youngest sister, and sobbed into his arm. When I asked if somebody had died, he lifted his head and showed me the picture.

"No," he said. "It is my sister. She was a baby when I left. Now look." She was ten in the picture, twelve when I met her. I saw the same hole in Mohammed Aduss's heart, but he closed it. "No," he said, wagging his finger, "he must finish school first."

※

The telephone rang and Mohammed shouted for Amira to get it. Neither he nor Mama ever answered the phone.

"Hello," Amira said. She listened, then looked at me, smiling broadly. "It is for you."

It was Ahmed. "Mom, is that you? Are you really there?"

"Yes, yes, Ahmed. I'm really here, in your house. Do you want to speak to your father?"

"No," he said. He wanted to talk to me first. "How are they? Is everybody all right?"

"They are wonderful," I said. "Really. Everybody is fine. They look wonderful."

"My mother?"

"Your mother is amazing. She is so strong. She works all the time."

"Everybody is fine?"

I could hear the relief in his voice. He didn't trust the family to tell him the truth. "They don't want to worry me," he told me before I left. "If something is wrong, they never tell me." But he believed me.

"You didn't tell me your house was so beautiful," I said.

"You like Harar?"

"I love it."

"How are you talking to them?"

I imagined him trying to imagine me sitting on the carpets, leaning against the green wall under the framed exhortations from the Qur'an. "Some English, some Amharic."

"My father is speaking English?"

"No, your sisters." I paused. "Your father *controls* everything though."

Ahmed laughed.

I looked at Mohammed watching me speak English to his son. "Your father is here, waiting to talk to you," I said and handed the phone to Mohammed. My job was done.

*

When I left Harar, Mohammed asked me to choose among the exquisite baskets that adorned the house. I protested; he insisted.

"For Ahmed," he said.

"For Ahmed," I said, and chose one.

"Take another," he said.

"One for Abdulnasser in Georgia," I said.

"And another."

"No," I said, "it is too many."

He insisted. I protested. How could I carry all those baskets home, much less to Kenya where I was going next? I refused adamantly. He insisted. I refused.

※

I left Harar with twenty-seven baskets, two kilos of *berbere*, a kilo of honey, and a pair of gold earrings in the shape of the Lion of Judah. I had been greeted as the prodigal son, with passionate kisses; I left as the obedient son, showered with gifts from the father who loved him.

Kathleen with Mohammed Aduss and Mama

First Grandchild

1

I see you only in pictures.
Your frowning face
against my daughter's arm,
Red and protesting your recent arrival,
surprised by your own, new birth.

Your wet brown hair reminds
me of the calf we saw born one Christmas Day
in Guy Hutchison's field down in Georgia.
We crested a hill—
your mother was there—
just as the hired man pulled out the calf,
wet and sleek as sausage.
As we watched the newborn struggle up to find its mother,
we couldn't believe we were standing in a field
with a miracle.
Now, your face is the same muscle of effort
straining toward my girl.

2

I remember when she couldn't drink from a cup.
I said that to her all the time when she was growing up,
so she would know how long I'd known her,
how well I knew her,
how much I loved her.
"I remember when you couldn't drink from a cup,"
I'd say.
"Oh, Mom," she'd say.

I did remember.

She'll be holding the cup to you soon,
six months or so—I don't remember when it comes—
you won't remember either,
but she will.

3

The two of you cause a lump to rise from my heart
and lodge in my throat,
so that everything that enters me
must know your presence.
You are the child of my child.

You must remember—
It was just last year that she was born,
last month she started school,
last week she fell in love.
Just yesterday you came.

4

When we saw that calf delivered
in a field of grass in Georgia,
your mother and I trembled,
mute and breathless at the miracle.
That's how it happens every time.
Birth and miracle in the same breath.

Now it's happened again
and I am breathless.

Follow the Child

When I was very young, I had questions that I instinctively knew were too weird, too strange, to say out loud.

Who, or what, was this thing inside me that thought and felt and spoke?

Who was this presence inside of me?

I went to Sunday school, heard about God and Jesus, but they seemed so separate from my questions of my own existence.

This wonder, the wonder of children is normal, is in us all if we protect it and let it rise, if we trust ourselves and trust the child.

Those thoughts made me wonder, not who am I, but what am I? And how did it happen, especially the unseen realm of thought and consciousness, how is it possible that I am here and thinking these . . . and many other thoughts? How is this consciousness, this "thinking" whatever it is, alive and present and speaking to me even—and especially—when I don't say a word, don't make a noise, am not even consciously thinking. The question, the inadequate question, is what, not who, but what am I. I haven't thought about this in many years, but as I remember my childish wondering, I realize I still don't have an answer.

I have the same question about the bird in today's picture in my Audubon calendar, the purple Scarlet Macaw. How did it come to be? (Yes, I know there are scientific explanations regarding creation and procreation, but really, how and from where did it all come?)

As I write these words, these old words, old questions, the feelings of wonder and amazement are there. Even the surprise at my hand writing the words almost as fast as I think them.

And what is thinking?

Does everybody have these thoughts?

Do birds? And cats? Dogs? Snails?

The poets surely do, and, I believe, children do as well. Children are the original bridegrooms married to amazement . . . if somebody doesn't kill that wonder first.

Transition

After six months in Kisumu, Chuck was transferred back to Nairobi to be Deputy Director. We moved into the house a departing staff member was leaving, hired her cook, wonderful William and, after we had been back in Nairobi for a few weeks, Kezieh let me know she had a son, Frank. Could Frank come and live with her.

Of course.

Frank was a wonderful addition to our household, a year older than Anna and her first friend and playmate.[10] And I too finally had a few friends, other staff wives, and eventually volunteered three hours a week at a girls' school run by the Salvation Army, but it wasn't enough.

I know I am not the only young mother who chafed under the loss of identity and purpose, exacerbated by not being needed in my own home:

Frank and Anna

---

10. Kezieh came to me one morning and told me that Anna, just over two years old, was speaking Kikuyu—ah, the brilliance of the child! Anna heard Kezieh and Frank talking with each other and figured out how to join in.

William cooked, Kezieh cleaned and took care of the children, and I? I wanted a real job, and that wasn't going to happen in Kenya. So, I was relieved when at the end of his Kenyan tour in the summer of 1971, Chuck turned down the opportunity to be Country Director in Malwai, and we moved back to Washington, D.C., where Chuck became the Deputy Director for the Africa Region.

We bought our first house and settled into a new kind of domestic life. Chuck's replacement in Kenya, also a former Peace Corps Volunteer, and his wife invited us for dinner so they could learn what life in Nairobi would be like for them and their three children. I hope we gave them helpful information, but I was the main beneficiary of that evening. Their children were just a few years older than Anna and John, and the mother in that family was a gifted researcher. She told me who the best pediatrician in town was, Dr. Alessio, and the best preschool, Mater Amoris Montessori School, which then was located not far from the house we had just bought near Chevy Chase Circle in Washington, D.C.

She was right on both counts. When Dr. Alessio entered the examining room, he had the gift of brightening with surprise and delight as if he were *particularly* thrilled to see that it was John or Anna waiting for him. He loved us, and we loved him right back.

My informant was right about the school too. I knew nothing of Montessori, had no idea what to expect or what to look for in a preschool, but called the school the next week. They accepted children as young as 2½ and had an opening for the next school year. Would I like to bring Anna in for an interview? They interviewed 2½ year olds! Yes, okay, I would.

Anna and I showed up at Mater Amoris the next week. We were smitten by the beauty of the school and the informative welcome by the head of the school. She made it clear that they were a school, not a day care center, a distinction I didn't really understand at the time, and took us on a tour. The classrooms were beautiful, bright and well-organized because, as I was to learn later, order and beauty are fundamental to Montessori's respect for children.

Transition

By the time John was admitted to Mater Amoris the following year, I was still floundering—what was I going to do with my life? Chuck had this great job—he was in Swaziland for six months that year, the children were thriving in their wonderful school, but what was *I* going to do, especially if we ended up in some exotic location? How was I going to prepare myself to have meaningful work wherever we lived?

The solution was right before me. If I took the Montessori training, became a Montessori guide (as Montessori teachers are called), I would be equipped to open a school in whatever exotic place we lived in next. I would always have work, real work, meaningful work, something that contributed to the family as well as to my need to be learning and growing.

The legislation creating the Peace Corps had stipulated that professional staff could only be employed by the agency for five years with the possibility of a one-year extension, which Chuck had received in order to fill a vital vacancy in Swaziland. After he returned from Swaziland, he worked as a consultant and was on the job market for a permanent position, interviewing for international as well as local positions. Our income stream was uncertain to say the least: we were paying tuition for both children at Mater Amoris, but Chuck generously supported my enrollment at the Washington Montessori Institute, the first, and at that time, the only Association Montessori Internationale[11] training program in the United States.

❋

An experience of awe and amazement precipitated by John, then three years old, solidified my decision to take the training.

Because the Phillips Collection had a much-touted Renoir exhibit that year, Anna's and John's classroom teachers had shown pictures of the paintings to their class, and both children came home talking

---

11. The Association Montessori Internationale (AMI) was founded by Dr. Montessori in 1929 to train teachers in what was becoming known as the Montessori Method.

about Renoir. So the following Saturday the four of us went to the museum to see the famed exhibit.

Renoir's *Luncheon of the Boating Party* was then and is now, a permanent part of the Phillips Collection. At 4 feet by more than 5-1/2 feet, the iconic painting is huge and was prominently displayed in a room at the end of a long hallway. John spotted it first, shouted "Luncheon of the Boating Party," ran for it, and skidded to a stop a foot away from the painting, pointing and exclaiming "Luncheon of the Boating Party" again and again in his three-year-old lisp.

Neither child touched the painting, or even reached for it, but an alarmed guard interceded immediately. She ordered us to hold them back and gave the distinct impression she would be most comfortable if we simply left the gallery, so we did. The children were heartbroken, and Chuck and I were angry. John broke into tears as soon as we were outside because he knew it was his fault, even though we told him again and again that it was *not* his fault, he had done nothing wrong. He knew. He knew he wasn't trusted.

A central Montessori tenet is "Trust the Child." After a year at Mater Amoris, our children had grown used to being trusted by people outside the family. It's not that they never made mistakes, or never gave in to a temptation to break that trust, but the *expectation* that you will be your best self is a powerful incentive to do and be just that, especially with something as spectacular as *Luncheon of the Boating Party*. John's first experience of the power of great art and his visible delight were shamed by lack of trust.

Straining for the Light

When we moved to exotic Minneapolis in 1974, I started a one-room school, Nokomis Montessori School. That first year, as a newly minted Montessori guide, I set up an experiment for my class of three-, four-, and five-year-olds to demonstrate that a plant needs good soil, water, and sunlight—all of it—to thrive.

The children planted the seeds in four pots: three of the pots lacked one essential element, soil, water, or light; the last pot had all three. I thought I knew what would happen—two of the beans would sprout: the one we put in a dark closet to deprive it of light and the one with water and soil on the windowsill—they both would sprout, but only the one on the windowsill would thrive. The pot without water and the pot without soil would fail to sprout.

We checked on them after a couple of weeks. The bean seed in the cup with no soil was bloated with water, but did indeed fail to sprout as did the seed in good light and soil, but no water. As I expected, the sprout on the windowsill was deep green, healthy, short—a sprout. The seed in the dark closet did indeed sprout—it was a long, pale string of a sprout, white with effort, desperately straining toward the light. To my chagrin, the children thought that was the successful one, pale and stringy, but look how big it was—several times longer than the other sprout. I don't remember how I turned them toward the better choice—*give* it light—but I learned and remembered, how every living thing strains towards the light, yearns for light, knows what it needs, and goes after it.

*

Two years before the bean seed fiasco, while we were still living in Washington, D.C., Anna had given me a lesson about the universality of straining for the light. She was three. We didn't go to church—I couldn't because I didn't believe what I had learned in my childhood and was put off by what I witnessed with missionaries in East Africa and had never even mentioned church to our kids. But children at school must have talked about going to church, and Anna wanted what others had.

Her need was genuine and great. She wanted to go to church, begged to go, so, eventually, I agreed. Chuck was out of town, so it was just the three of us, Anna, age four, John, three, and me, dressed for church one Sunday morning.

As we walked to the car, Anna said, heavy with disappointment, "You're wearing that?" The only picture she'd ever seen of me in church was of our wedding, with me in a long, white dress studded with pearls. That fancy dress was part of the mystery for her.

We arrived at the church early, *very* early, because I was shy and nervous. The usher made us feel welcome, but I knew we didn't belong, and I chose to sit in the very last pew with the two children. We were so early that the sanctuary was nearly empty, and quiet, then, after ten minutes or so, the organist began, and thundering music filled the room.

Anna grabbed my arm. "Is that God?" she said.

That was her hunger—for the mystery, for the holy, for the sacred; it was her very human yearning for the light. Three years old, and she was straining for it.

But I couldn't give her the God of my childhood, with or without the vestment of my wedding dress, but still she yearned for that experience of the mystery, the light, the sacred, the holy—because she was human, and we weren't providing it. She knew enough to ask for it—it's what humans do and want—and that yearning is about faith, not about belief. Not creed, but mystery, amazement, the holy.

※

Anna didn't give up. Three years later, when she was six, she asked if we were Jewish. We had made it clear that we weren't Christian, and I had responded to a lot of questions in those days with the words, "Some people believe, but . . ." By then, she was aware of other possibilities. Maybe we were Jewish, but just hadn't remembered to tell her. She was asking what path *we* were on, and I still didn't have an answer. It was embarrassing not to have a clear answer to give my own children.

Well, maybe we were Quakers; we could try that. So one Sunday Chuck and I and the two children drove to the Friends Meeting House in Minneapolis. It was just before 11:00 a.m, but the service had started at 10:30 a.m. We couldn't possibly walk in half an hour late, so we turned for home, embarrassed in front of our children, unable—again—to answer that most basic question: Who are we? Where do we place our heart? What do we have faith in?

We were almost home when we paused at a church we had passed many times, First Universalist Church, a church and a denomination we knew nothing about. The sign in front said the sermon that morning was "Why I am a Unitarian Universalist." Well, the children were expecting something from us, *anything*, the service hadn't started yet, and we might learn something, so we parked the car and went in. Somebody greeted us at the door, took charge of the children for Sunday school, and Chuck and I found inconspicuous seats in the back just as the music started.

It began as expected, music, an offering, people of a variety of ages, and according to the sign in front, the Reverend John Cummins would be explaining what Unitarian Universalism was. Great.

Which is what he did. "It is only a love that is all inclusive, large in its world view, without reservation or defense, that will not calculate or bargain, that will be healing enough and universal enough to meet the need of the whole human family... It is not the way of Christ or nothing, followed by life everlasting, but the way of life itself. It is to be concerned both for those who do harm and for those who suffer it..."[12] This illumined something in me, offered a possible answer to Anna's persistent questions.

Reverend Cummins went on to say, "Do you still believe in Santa Claus as you did as a child? Of course you don't! You have rejected the old, the childish faith in a literal Santa to make room for a larger, albeit more abstract faith in the rightness, joy, and goodness of giving. You have become an atheist with regard to Santa Claus, and yet you now possess a larger faith than ever before... we all become atheists with regard to lesser beliefs as we outgrow and replace them with larger ones. It is a terrible mistake to categorize others who happen to be at a different place in their religious development than our own. To avow anything at any time of life is to disavow others. Real religion is a living, growing thing... On the living tree of life, small branches of conviction shoot out, often in unproductive directions, die and are trimmed away, while others, starting out as small notions, become great, supporting branches; but always the tree itself is reaching toward the light."[13]

These religious words—faith, God, prayer, even church and religion—had been roadblocks for me, triggered a negative response, but we returned again and again to First Universalist, became members, and are still there nearly fifty years later. I have learned to accept all those words, sometimes making mental substitutions when I need to. I don't believe in the God of my childhood who I thought might

---

12. Why I am a Unitarian Universalist, the Reverend John Cummins, 1975.
13. Ibid.

intervene directly in my life if I asked him right, if I were good, if I prayed. But I am reaching toward the light, have faith in the holy, the sacred, the mystery, the connection between me and the life I can't see or define.

※

Often, we have to substitute words for the meaning to speak to us, to help us come out of the religious closet, so to speak. I learned our family's favorite table blessing from a friend who is Catholic. Her family begins with the words, "Creator God, give us a heart for simple things . . ." I shift it to "Spirit of Life," but the rest resonates with me: "Give us a heart for simple things, love and laughter, bread and wine, tales and dreams. Fill our hearts with green and growing hope; make us a people of justice whose song is alleluia and whose name breathes love." *Amen*, she says. *So be it*, I say.

There is faith, and then there is belief. Belief makes me change those words from Creator God to Spirit of Life; faith, that turning toward the light, embraces the rest of the blessing. We are reaching for the same thing.

※

So, at eighty-one, I'm still reaching toward the light, still growing. Sometimes I feel like that pale, stringy bean plant, straining for all I'm worth, and not finding enough. Then I discover some beam of light, of beauty, of belief, of grace and amazement, and I know that everybody in churches, synagogues, mosques, stupas, temples, on the sidewalk out front, down the street, across the nation, and around the world is with me on the stalk, at different places, but it is a sturdy, powerful plant with room for everybody—Christians, Muslims, Buddhists, Jews, atheists, idolators, the churched and the unchurched. All of us are straining toward the light, different in our understanding, in our beliefs, but straining is the practice of faith. "Faith is love taking the form of aspiration."[14]

I know that is true because a child showed me more than fifty years ago when the organ sounded. *Is that God?*

I should have said, "Yes, Anna, that is God. That is the holy, that is love, that is the source of light we are yearning for, the light we are leaning into, the spirit of life. You are straining toward the holy; I am bending towards the light; we all are, in our own way, in faith. And it is amazing."

---

14. The Reverend Justin Schroeder's answer when I asked him why he signed his emails "*In Faith.*"

Discovery of the Child

When I opened my one-room Montessori school, I rented a room in Nokomis Heights Lutheran Church and called the school Nokomis Montessori School. I created brochures using Anna, John, and a friend's children as "models" in the brochure, leafletted the near-by neighborhood and was pleased . . . and relieved . . . to open with ten students in January of 1975—hardly enough to support the cost of the school, but a start.

I expanded my leafletting range that summer and, with the help of Anna and John, left brochures at a thousand houses, so by fall I had enough students for a real class, and with more than 20 children needed another adult in the room. I advertised for a Spanish or French speaking person and happily, Beth, a fluent Spanish speaker, applied for the job.

Montessori describes the young child's gift for learning as the "absorbent mind," the innate ability to soak up everything in her environment, and I remembered Anna speaking Kikuyu with Kezieh and Frank. Beth spoke only Spanish in all her interactions in the classroom and, when appropriate, offered Spanish lessons to an individual child or a small group. The children were unfazed by her apparent inability to speak or understand English.[15]

Montessori described the powerful ability of young children to concentrate when they were engaged in something that interested them, when they were engaged in an activity that was meaningful to them and said the role of the adult was to observe the child and to follow the child. Scientist that she was, she observed what brought the children joy and comfort, what was upsetting and learned to, in her words, "follow the child." She learned to ferret out what the children needed by observation, not by what she thought they needed, but what she *observed* they needed. This was her "discovery of the child" and primary among her discoveries was the child's need for independence and meaningful work . . . and that there are times in the development of the human child that she is particularly sensitive to language, to order, to mathematics, to color, to discovery of the world around them—revolutionary views in 1905.

During my training to be a Montessori teacher, I spent a week, five consecutive mornings, in each of six Montessori classrooms, observing the children and taking copious notes, because knowing how to observe is a basic skill and expectation of a Montessori guide. Every guide spends part of the day, every day, taking notes, observing who needs what or is ready for a lesson, but not interfering when children are productively engaged.[16]

One example I often used when talking to parents was the child who needed help threading a needle. (Sewing was always a popular "work" in my classrooms, among both boys and girls.) If the child was struggling to thread her needle, she could wait patiently if the guide was busy with another child or she could go to an older child, a

---

15. Montessori was clear that there should be only one "teacher" or guide in the classroom—too many adults "teaching" robbed the children of their independence and discovery on their own. A second adult helped a child when asked, and made sure the environment was orderly and accessible to everybody, but other than Spanish, Beth didn't offer lessons or presentations that I did as the guide.

16. Being "engaged" includes respectfully watching another child, walking around, looking at things, maybe just watching others before making a choice for oneself.

five-year-old, and ask for help. If the guide interrupted herself, quickly took the needle from the child, and threaded it, all the child would have would be a threaded needle, but not the satisfaction and experience of learning how to solve the problem. Asking another child, waiting patiently until the guide finished what she was doing, or even managing to thread it herself after a bit of a struggle is the expectation.[17]

Montessori also talked about children's deep concentration when involved in an activity that was meaningful to them. I am sure I wasn't the only guide who didn't always experience the level of concentration she described in my classroom. There were times, certainly, when an individual child would demonstrate a deeper level of focus, but seldom as often or as profoundly as Montessori described.

That is until Alex. We returned from Colombia in mid-March and he joined my class of three-to six-year-olds for the rest of that school year. He learned English quickly, but it was the variety of materials in the classroom that attracted him, that held his attention, that he couldn't get enough of. I gave him several lessons at the beginning because it was all so new to him, and he was entering late in the year when the other children were well acquainted with the rhythm of the classroom. That said, he approached every day, every presentation, every material with a level of concentration and focus that I hadn't seen in many (if any) other children. When I think of him now, I see him bent over the math material called the long rods, ordering them by length, counting the alternating blue and red stripes, and placing the cards with the number indicating their length. He focused on his work and was oblivious to what was going on in the rest of the room, concentrating deeply, exactly as Montessori had described, *actively* engaged in constructing himself.[18]

---

17. That is only one small example of Montessori's respect for the human need for autonomy and that the most powerful growth and learning comes when we figure out how to solve a problem.

18. Unlike the other children, Alex didn't yet have a bedroom full of toys, no Fisher Price gas stations, no box full of matchbox cars, no Legos or puzzles. He would acquire that furniture of an American childhood, but he still had the gift of focus and concentration.

❊

I remembered Alex's gift for deep focus and concentration when, nearly thirty years later, his son Beck, age five, created an activity for himself in his Montessori classroom that no guide would suggest because of the difficulty and complexity. Luckily the guide recognized his interest and independence and let him proceed without interruption.

The beautiful wooden puzzle maps are a fixture in every Montessori environment. The map of the world, with the seven continents, is the first one offered to a child, then the map of the child's continent, North America with its twenty-three countries for Beck, then the puzzle maps of the other continents, and, finally, the puzzle map of the child's own country divided into states or provinces, fifty pieces for an American child.

On this day, Beck took the puzzle map of each continent, the twenty-three countries of North America, twelve in South America, the fifty in Europe, etc., and created his own enormous puzzle map of the world on the floor, with the more than one hundred-ninety countries placed in proper relationship to each other. It was such a complex task that no teacher would suggest it or introduce it to a five-year old, but Beck's teacher trusted him, and the other children knew to walk around his massive project. I am guessing that several children sat and watched him, but they knew not to interrupt. It took him three hours, but he did it, did it himself.

Trust the child.
Follow the child.[19]

❊

---

19. Lest this sound too idealistic and unworkable, guides quickly intervene if somebody might be hurt or a child isn't able to respect other children or the materials. It takes some children weeks or even months to "get" how the classroom functions, to understand the boundaries, and to manage their own impulses in respect for their peers.

I feel compelled at this point to mention that Alex did grow up to be a "normal" American teenager and a highly competent adult.

When all the kids were in their teens, I made a Saturday job list for each child to sign up for, tasks such as: clean the upstairs bathroom, vacuum and dust the living room, vacuum the stairs and second floor landing, clean and replace the cat litter, sweep and damp mop the kitchen floor. Each child was expected to sign up for a job by breakfast time and to complete their job before doing anything else that day. It was part of being a member of the family.

Alex was fifteen or sixteen when he complained, "The only reason you had children was so we would clean the house!"

Using admirable restraint (in my opinion), I did *not* point out that that these jobs would be *much* simpler if there weren't five teenagers in the house. (Alex always chose the bathroom, and, I am happy to say, he was thorough and competent at leaving it bright and sparkling.)

Poetry by Heart

When my grandchildren were young, I paid them to memorize poetry.

My mother did it—paid my brother and me a dime for "Grass," a quarter for "O Captain, My Captain," thirty-five cents for "Sea Fever." It was the fifties, we were on the school's winter break, driving from Georgia to California, five days each way, and missing a week of school. It was educational, she said, and the money we earned would be our vacation spending money. It was also a strategy to keep us from arguing over who crossed the imaginary line in the back seat of the car.

We made it to Los Angeles and back in relative peace and with sufficient funds for cheap souvenirs, so it worked. My mother was a practical woman, but she also loved language and knew what she was doing. I don't remember what I bought with those dimes and quarters, but I still have the poetry deep in my heart. Sixty years later, I can close my eyes and the words come rising in my throat.

Which is why I paid my grandchildren to memorize poetry when they were young. Like my mother, I, too, believe in the power of language to soothe and heal; to inspire, to calm. Poetry is to be spoken aloud, learned by heart; a poem spoken in the music of your own voice becomes a part of you, and if you learn it when you are young, you will have it forever.

At Thanksgiving one year, I gave each child a book of poetry, told them the story of my mother's payment plan, recited de Regniers' "Keep a Poem in Your Pocket" ("and a picture in your head/and you'll never feel lonely/at night when you're in bed") and promised to pay up whenever they learned a new poem.

That was on a Thursday. Friday morning, Beck, then five, appeared at his parents' bedside to recite Stevenson's "Birdie with a Yellow Bill." They had read it to him the night before, and he had taken de Regniers' advice to heart. Beck often had trouble sleeping and knew what it was to feel lonely at night when he was in bed, so he said the poem to himself, over and over, until he fell asleep.

At five, Beck discovered what poets and mystics have known for centuries: Be present to the moment, give yourself over to the rhythm and mystery of your own voice, lose yourself in the hum of the words, and you will find that quiet place within. The little poem was a mantra for him, a chant, a meditation. The rhythmic combination of sound and sense slowed his fluttering heart and lulled him to sleep. He ran to tell his parents because he had just discovered that the most fundamental gift of our species, language, has the power to communicate inward as well as outward.

I gave him a dollar (2008 rates), and I made several payments to my other grandchildren over the next few years. They all seemed more interested in "the little poem [that] sings to you" than the money earned. That Christmas, we heard "Jabberwocky," "Tyger, Tyger," "Stopping by the Woods on a Snowy Evening," "The Man That Wasn't There," and, of course, "A Birdie with a Yellow Bill." Nobody asked how much their poem was worth, because they already knew. Money may have been the carrot, but it is love that keeps "a poem in your pocket and a picture in your head."

Higher Calling

There's an old *New Yorker* cover (August 3, 1998) that shows four adults at the beach, all bent over with phones in their ears. A child in the foreground holds a conch shell to her ear and is smiling with delight. The adults are us, of course, intent on what has to be done, even at the beach, checking items off their list and charging forward. The child is herself, completely enraptured with this marvelous planet she has found herself on, engaged with the smallest pleasures, focused and ready to hear the call of the universe and able to see rapture and beauty in the ordinary and in the daily. This is the child we are working with, all of us, parents and teachers, and we need to remember their gifts every day.

The child is full of wonder and delight, curiosity, and a million questions.

The child is alive to the possibilities of the universe and is ready to receive what is there to be offered. It's not that laptops and cell phones are bad; they aren't. They are the tools of our daily world.

But the child is interested in the fundamental nature of things, in shells and the sand and the water and all the fish of the sea. That is who she is. She is fascinated with language and numbers, and the way things work. It is this interest and this engagement that inspires her to read, to do long division, to draw, and to make music. It is this path, through the conch shell, that leads her to be her best self.

When children have the shell pressed to their ears, they hear a higher calling, the call of the universe. It is our job to preserve that smile of delight and that deep engagement with the universe.

Second Time Around

I've climbed the Eiffel Tower, seen David in Florence, strolled the beach in Menorca, hiked the West Highland Way in Scotland, walked to Santiago and been lucky as a tourist, but nothing lingers or resonates like the weeks or months when I lived in a new place, had a job, learned a bit of a new language, ate strange food, made mistakes, and made friends.

Matatu

At fifty, I had a grant to return to East Africa, to get in touch with the places that populated the stories I was writing then. I traveled there with more time than money and depended on local buses, trains, and, my personal favorite, *matatus*. *Matatus* are pickup trucks held together by luck and will, packed with passengers beyond any reasonable capacity, and that travel at terrifying speeds. I'd done it before, was used to it, and liked the intimacy of strangers riding thigh to thigh with no place to look but at one another's faces.

Every time I took a *matatu* I expected to crash, so I memorized the other passengers—the Masai woman wearing a beaded choker like a neck brace, the old mama chewing some leaf with the sweet aroma of compost, the guy in the suit balancing his wrists on the points of his knees so his sleeves wouldn't wrinkle, and I'd think, if this is my day, here's a group I could go out with.

I was in a *matatu* in Uganda, and the guy on my left was smuggling sugar in from Kenya. I didn't know this until he dived out the window at a roadblock. He froze in the middle of the road for a moment, eyes darting, then dashed down a gully and disappeared into the woods. The woman next to me slipped a kilo of the contraband sugar into her basket, then pulled my skirt over the rest just as a soldier stuck his semiautomatic in the window.

The *matatu* was packed with people, but the soldier had eyes for me alone. I was the only foreigner.

"Passport?"

He took it, looked at my picture, looked at me, back and forth three times, then handed it back and walked away.

That's why I travel. I don't know what's going on, and I'm in the middle of it.

Mwembe's Woman

I arrived at Whispering Palms Hotel sweat-streaked and on foot, with a duffel bag on my back, but the guard let me pass through the first gate anyway. My age and white skin were enough to get me in, but my general condition made a uniformed man chase after me before I reached the graceful entrance with its fountains and statues. "Can I help you, Madam?"

"Yes. I'm looking for the Cantina," I said. "Mwembe and Njoroge."

"It is there," he said, turning me around with a touch to my elbow. "On the road."

I walked back to the gate, nodded to the guard, and continued another hundred yards to a round cement-block building that served as a snack bar and dance hall for hotel workers. The Cantina. Several young Kenyan men lounged at one of the long picnic tables watching a buxom woman in an oversized Alpha Tau Omega T-shirt sweep the floor with a broom that was so short, she was forced to stoop double. In spite of her hunched posture, she smoked, swept in time to Kenny Rogers singing "Lucille" on the jukebox, danced a step or two, and carried on a conversation that embraced everybody in the room. When I appeared, she stuck the truncated broom under her arm and straightened up to observe my entrance. Everybody stopped talking. I hesitated in the middle of the room, wondered who to approach first, and was adjusting the slippery weight of the duffel bag on my back, when a skinny, grinning teenager hurried over with his hand out. "Can I help you?" he said.

I let the duffel slide to the floor. "Yes. I am looking for Mwembe or Njoroge. Maria sent me."

At the mention of Maria, he broke into a beatific smile. "This is wonderful," he said. "I am him. I am Njoroge."

He grabbed my bag and hoisted it to his shoulder. "Come, come," he said and took my arm as he would for a long-absent, beloved friend. "We will find Mwembe."

I was parched and exhausted—I had just walked 6 kilometers under a relentless sun. I would have preferred to rest for a minute and get something to drink, but he quickly shepherded me out the door, across the road, and down a footpath ankle-deep in sand. The path was shaded by columns of coconut palms and looked inviting, but it was terrifically hot. After a few minutes Njoroge was clearly struggling with my duffle bag. "You carried this?" he gasped.

"Yes," I said. I took a handle and we squeezed together to carry the bag along the narrow path. It was a path I would walk many times in the next ten days. Once I stopped and looked around, wondering if I should take a picture of it, should try to capture what a walk through a coconut palm forest on the way to the village of Kikambala is like. I didn't take the picture because it would never show enough: the deep sand, the fifty-foot-high coconut palms, the underbrush of crashed palm fronds, coconut shells scattered across the sand, the pokes of light through the trees. It was shady and quiet without being comfortable. So hot and dry in the sand. Writing this now, in northern Minnesota in December, I am struck again with how walking through that coconut palm forest was like walking through the northern woods among the jack pine full of snow. Quiet. White. Spikes of sun through the trees. Rustle high up. Monkeys in the trees instead of chickadees. So hot there. So cold here.

A coconut crashed to the ground just in front of us with the force of a bowling ball falling a hundred feet. "Yikes," I said. "What was that?"

Njoroge laughed. "A coconut from up there." He pointed with his chin.

"That could kill you. Aren't they dangerous?"

He thought it was a hilarious question. "No. Nothing ever happens with them. We eat them."

We passed what looked like random clusters of huts and rectangular buildings scattered in no pattern that I could discern, along no path, facing at odd angles to one another: the village.

Just ahead, a man was sawing a board that leaned against a tree. When he spotted us, he dropped the saw and hurried over. He was disarmingly handsome, with flawless ebony skin, a taut bony face, and a blinding smile. Mwembe. He was broader than Njoroge, taller, a man, not a boy. He laughed when I told him Maria sent me, and I wanted to stay with them, that I wanted to live in a hut, wanted to learn about the village, just as Maria had.

"This is good," he said. "Very wonderful."

"She has sent you a letter and some other things."

They took me to a long, corrugated tin building, one room wide, with four doors and a cement slab across the front. Mwembe unlocked the padlock on the end door and we went in. It was a small room, six by ten, separated from the next room by a 7-foot high divider. There was no ceiling. The room was open to the thatched roof and branches used as studs which supported the tin walls on the inside. It seemed to be a kind of closet or storeroom: a couple of cardboard boxes on the floor contained a jumble of miscellaneous items; a narrow pad on a piece of plywood was covered by a bed sheet so thin the blue flowers looked like shadows, and a wire strung above the pad held an assortment of rags and clothes.

Mwembe and Njoroge sat down and opened Maria's letter and package. They immediately ate the candy she sent, then exclaimed over the letter and admired the socks and shorts. As I watched them,

I gradually realized that the pad was a mattress and the "storeroom" was their home, where the two of them lived together, and, as it turned out, where I was to live for the next ten days. There were no huts to rent.

✻

I went to Kikambala in an attempt to connect with "Kenyan life." I'd been writing stories about white women in Africa, but I hadn't been there in twenty years. I needed to know if I was getting it right, if the texture of life was as I remembered it. When I came home, people asked me if I'd found what I'd gone for and were confused when I didn't have a definitive answer. I'd been away for three months—either I had found it or I hadn't.

It wasn't that simple. I wasn't an anthropologist taking notes on courting rituals; I wasn't after facts or patterns or oral histories, but the fabric of stories, the kind you make up, not the kind you record. I could have taped the stories Mwembe and Njoroge told me—they think in story the way I do—but I wasn't after their stories. I was looking for my own.

My ten days there were as idyllic as they were confusing. The days were idyllic because of Mwembe's enormous capacity for generosity and friendship and because of the profound simplicity of daily life in Kikambala. We lived in the air there, in the heat and the rain, with raucous monkeys, marauding goats, foraging chickens; we lived with sweat and constant physical labor to accomplish the simplest tasks. Illness and death were as close as the stars at night and the first piercing rays of the sun at dawn.

When I went for a last word with Mama Hashima before leaving, the feisty old lady who gossiped with us on the slab most nights, she was so ill she couldn't raise her head. "We must do something," I said to Mwembe, but he shrugged. She had malaria, so of course, she was weak. I couldn't accept her illness, but it didn't occur to Mwembe to question it.

I had to be taught everything: how to chop an onion in my hand, how to cook beans over a fire, how to draw water from a well, even how to sit without moving or speaking and watch the clouds drift across the night sky, switching off the stars as if they were light bulbs, until the envelope of dark swallowed every part of us, and it was time to sleep. Learning to live in Kikambala was like recovering from a long illness when you learn again to do what some stirring of the unconscious tells you you once did naturally.

The confusion came from the presence of three elegant beach hotels nearby and the profound effect the steady influx of tourists in search of exotic experiences had on the village economy. It took me a day or so to realize that many of the hotel guests were more interested in an exotic sexual adventure than an Indian Ocean tan and that, in the minds of the villagers, I was lumped with the most adventurous foreigners—I was living in Mwembe's room.

It seemed clear that neither Mwembe nor Njoroge expected anything from me that I didn't want to give. I had been sent by our mutual friend, Maria, but she hadn't told me she met Mwembe when she was a guest in the hotel or that she moved into his room *with* him. Mwembe showed me photographs of him and Maria with their arms around each other and her head on his shoulder. "I want to marry a tourist," he explained.

※

There was no place for my things in the room. Mwembe emptied the largest cardboard box and put it on the floor in the back corner. "For you," he said and left me alone to unpack.

He was waiting when I came out. "Can you wash your body with your hands?"

"Yes," I said. I didn't know what he meant, but I was ready for my own version of the exotic.

A woman appeared just then with a plastic basin full of water. I didn't realize until much later that Mwembe had ordered her to go to the well to draw my bath. She placed the basin on the ground behind a three-walled lean-to. I was embarrassed by the special service, but was so hot from my trek in that I couldn't bring myself to refuse the bath. I hung my dress over the gap in the lean-to and squatted at the basin to cup the water in my hands. I let it trickle over my skin and back into the basin a few times, then added soap and did a final rinse. I had no towel, but it was so hot that my skin dried while I rinsed my hair with the last drops of water. My pleasure in husbanding the water so that each drop was individually absorbed by my parched body was palpable. I wasted nothing. I washed my body with my hands.

*

The woman who brought the water lived in the room next to mine with her two daughters: Pando, who looked to be about three, and Happy, a baby who had an American father, according to Mwembe.

"Oh, where is he from? What is his name?"

Mwembe didn't know. He didn't know the mother's name either, so I thought of her as Helen, after Helen of Troy, because she was so lovely—square face, high cheekbones, and perfect teeth. Most days, Helen wore a red *kanga* bordered in black and green with the words SORRY FATHER repeated along the border and a pale gray blouse splotched with white flowers like bedroom wallpaper. She wove a couple of yellow beads into her braid, threaded wire through the holes in her ears, and wore blue and yellow beads on a string around her neck. The one time she left the village, she put on a tailored skirt and a white blouse that made her look like a particularly elegant stenographer.

She slept alone most nights but had a lover who appeared every three or four days, a gaunt man who always wore a long wool overcoat in spite of the heat. The overcoat was the uniform of his profession—he worked as a night watchman for a German in a big house on the beach.

Mwembe said the man was a deserter from the Kenyan army who fled when all his companions were killed by Somalis on the frontier.

"We couldn't see where the bullets were coming from. They lay in the sand like fish on the bottom of the sea, and they killed us." Helen and the deserter tried to be quiet when he spent the night, but I heard them anyway.

Another woman lived in the third room with her husband and her baby boy, Tieno. This woman did nothing but sit on the cement slab in front of the house with her baby and ask me to give her things—the blouse I was wearing, my *kanga*, my bag, my skirt. She had huge, pendulous breasts that hung to her navel. I went swimming the third day and hung my swimsuit to dry on a tree behind the house, and she took it. I wondered how she'd get those huge breasts in my skimpy suit.

A white-haired man lived in the last room. He mumbled in his sleep at night, but that was the only time I heard him speak. He was gone during the day and in the evening he sat alone at the end of the cement porch.

By the time I got up at 7 a.m. every morning, Helen had swept the compound in front of all our doors, been to the well for water, washed her own patch of cement, scoured the surrounding area for coconuts and palm fronds that had dropped in the night and dragged them in front of her door to weave into thatch later that day, and was washing Happy with detergent in a basin of water.

She supported herself and her children by selling the thatch she wove to local hut and house contractors. She sat on the ground with Happy on her back and cut lengths from palm fronds with a long machete-like knife called a *panga*. She stripped the leaves from the stalk, then hacked the stalk into three- or four-foot strips. Meanwhile, she soaked fibrous stalks that she would use to weave it all together.

Pando cut palm stalks with a *panga* just like her mother; she cut small lengths, Helen long ones. Then they sat side by side, their backs straight as trees, held the stalks steady between their toes, and wove thatch. The two of them talked and sang as they worked, but their hands never stopped. Happy either slept tied to Helen's back or babbled to himself in a cardboard box that Mwembe had given Helen to use as a playpen.

At night, I switched the padlock from outside the door to inside and locked it. Mwembe told me never to open the door to anybody. "Trust no man," he said.

I felt a little like Snow White, but I was touched by his solicitude and agreed not to open the door when they were away. It was beach boys that he was cautioning me against. "I want to marry a tourist," Mwembe had told me the first day, "but I am not a beach boy. Oh, no, ask any man. Njoroge and I are not beach boys. But I want to marry a tourist."

He was clearly disappointed when I told him I was married, but he brightened up considerably when I mentioned my twenty-year-old daughter. "Yes, I want to see her," he said. He was twenty-two.

Njoroge was living with Mwembe because Njoroge's older brother's house had burned down some months earlier and Njoroge had had to give up his house to this brother. They both told me, in separate conversations, that the brother, who was married and had a child, hadn't rebuilt his own house because he was a beach boy, which I took to mean that he was lazy and got money too easily.

When they talked about beach boys, I imagined handsome youths in cutoff jeans and straw hats, probably barefoot or in Ho Chi Minh sandals, selling shells and seducing women, so I was surprised, and a little disappointed, when I met my first beach boy. He arrived on a girl's bicycle with the same straw basket swinging from the handlebars that I had on my Schwinn thirty years earlier. It made him seem childish instead of alluring. His name was Gordon, and he was dressed in khaki shorts and a freshly pressed white shirt. He had what you would call a famous smile—all teeth and enthusiasm and, although he wasn't particularly good looking, he was charming: delighted to meet me, incredulous at his luck, couldn't have been happier. He made Mwembe promise to bring me to his house and to his shop as soon as possible, then established something of a conspiratorial relationship with me. "When will you finish my bed?" he asked Mwembe and winked at me.

Mwembe shrugged. "Soon."

"This boy, I have much work for him. Much work," Gordon said, "but he is lazy. If he will come to my place, I have much work for him. You tell him to come."

I smiled, nodded, said that I would, and wondered why Mwembe had not followed through on this work. He obviously needed the money.

The beach boy shook my hand again with both of his and told me how very pleased he was that I was in his village. He couldn't wait to see me again.

"He didn't seem so bad," I said to Mwembe as Gordon pedaled off. "He was nice."

Mwembe frowned. "He wants you to stay at his house, but it's not good. Not good." He shook his head. "I tell him you are staying here, with me."

"I am fine here," I said, "but where are you and Njoroge sleeping?"

"We have two places, two rooms we can sleep in."

I had arrived in Kikambala thinking I could rent a room or hut, but there was nothing available, or so Mwembe had said. The longer I was there, the more I realized that nothing was as it seemed. I now think it would have been possible for me to get my own place, but Mwembe had a proprietary interest in me because of the honor my visit brought him.

Gordon returned the next day and, reluctantly, Mwembe agreed to let me go to Gordon's house, but only under his escort. We followed Gordon through the village, past Whispering Palms Hotel, and up a dry, unshaded hill to a four-room cement-block house with glass windows and a thatched roof. "See my big house," he said. In the third room on our tour of the house, we came upon his mother, a squat, bent woman who greeted me automatically but without the expressive enthusiasm of her son. I belatedly realized she was blind and wished I had taken her hand or arm and tried to speak Swahili with her.

The fourth room was furnished with a horsehair sofa, the underpinnings of which protruded like extra toes, a coffee table, and two metal folding chairs. A fat white woman whose legs had been piped like dough into orange capri pants sprawled on the sofa with a Kenyan man in shorts. The man greeted Mwembe and glanced at me. The woman kept her eyes at knee level.

"Hi," I said. Neither of them responded.

I refused the beer Gordon offered, so he brought me a Coke. Mwembe and I perched on the edge of the metal chairs while I drank the warm Coke and Gordon described his plans for me: he would show me many things, he would be my guide, we would go to Fort Jesus. "We shall go to disco, everything, yes?" He smiled his famous smile.

The white woman suddenly heaved herself up, left the room, then returned with a beer for the other man, which he took with a nod. The blind mother shuffled in, patting the wall with the side of one hand. All the chairs were taken, which gave Mwembe and me the perfect opportunity to vacate ours. We jumped up, thanked Gordon for his hospitality, and fled.

"Who was that other man?" I asked.

"Gordon's brother. Another beach boy."

"And the woman?"

"His wife." Mwembe shrugged. "She has an old husband in Germany, but she comes here every year for three weeks."

※

The next night Helen brought over octopus and a plate of *ugali*[20]. She said I needed some real *ugali*. The day before she'd brought cassava boiled in coconut milk; it was exquisite food, simply prepared.

Later, Mama Hashima from the hut behind our house joined us on the porch along with Helen and the deserter. Tien's father and the old man sat at the end and smoked. Everybody else joked and laughed together in Swahili. I could follow the conversation enough to nod occasionally, but, at one point, they were laughing so hysterically I had to ask Mwembe to translate. "It is the tourists at the hotel," he explained. "The

---

20. Ugali is a type of cornmeal made from maize or corn flour. It is cooked in boiling water or milk until it reaches a stiff or firm dough-like consistency.

men want to buy boys." He repeated it in Swahili and Mama Hashima put her head in her lap and cackled over that one for a long time.

※

There was a small, low table at the head of the bed where I left money. The boys took it to buy food, water, and mosquito coils; they put the change on the table, and we left it there until it was needed again. The basic food supplies—salt, sugar, coffee, and bread—were stored in a small cardboard box, along with the matches and paraffin for the stove. There was a second box with a pot for cooking, three plastic bowls, three forks, one large spoon, two small spoons, two plastic cups, and two brown ceramic cups.

There was one butter knife and one sharp knife. I kept cutting myself with the sharp knife because it was so wobbly and dull and there was no surface to cut on. I couldn't peel and slice fruits and vegetables in my hand the way Mwembe could. He separated slices of mango from the hairy seed and offered them on the end of the knife like slivers of glistening sapphire. He handled papaya the same way, each perfect slice could have been plucked from a painting.

The third time I cut myself he snatched the knife out of my hand. "I'm going to kill this. It's *kali* for you."

"No, it's okay," I said. "A sharp knife is better than a dull one."

"No, it is *kali*," he said and ground the thin blade against the edge of the cement slab we were sitting on to dull and nick it.

"Stop," I said. "You're ruining the knife."

He didn't stop until it was too notched and scarred to cut anything. He didn't want to see my blood again.

I wanted to say, look, I am the mother of five and in my own kitchen I'm a whiz with knives, mixers, blenders, microwaves, garbage disposals, turning stoves on and off, and cleaning toasters. I can even handle an electric knife.

The night I cooked for them, I made chili and fruit salad with store-bought sliced white bread on the side. The beans were pebbly and the fruit butchered rather than sliced. Fortunately, it took me so long to prepare the meal that it was too dark for us to see what we were eating by the time I served it. It was the worst meal I ate in Kikambala.

We ate all our meals outside on the cement slab. The other families on our "slab" didn't—they ate in their dark rooms with the door open so they could see—but Mwembe, Njoroge, and I sat in front of our door and ate out of the same bowl with our three spoons.

※

We were leaning against the wall of the house, eating bread and bananas for breakfast one day, when Mwembe spied a boy passing on the path that led to the *duka*[21]. The child looked to be four years old.

"Shadrach," Mwembe called, "where are you going this morning?"

Shadrach stopped, put his hand under the elastic of his shorts, and turned his head, but not his shoulder, toward the sound of Mwembe's voice. He was frozen on the path.

"*Jambo,* Shadrach. *Habari?*"

The child squirmed, raised each big toe, folded the left toe on top of the right, and stretched his neck like a crane at sunrise.

"Come. Have some banana."

Shadrach put his other hand in his shorts and balled his fists together so it looked as if a tiny tumor had popped from his navel. His head didn't move, but the small body clenched and unclenched at the sound of Mwembe's voice.

"He's afraid," I said. "Let him go."

"But I like this boy," Mwembe said. "I like his head. He has a beautiful head."

Shadrach's head was an elongated ovoid. His small, rounded chin widened to a perfect, close-cut dome. His ears curved tightly around his scalp, a calyx cupping the perfect flower. His solemn mouth and shaded eyes were limned across the shell of his skull.

---

21. *Duka* is the Swahili word for shop or store.

"Where are you going?" Mwembe called again.

Shadrach's perfect chin flickered, pointing down the path.

"Go then. Go to the *duka*[22] for your mother."

I expected him to break into a run when he was released by Mwembe's friendly voice, but his left foot slowly lifted off his right, his knee bent, the right foot moved, the heel shimmered, and he inched down the path again, the shy boy with the beautiful skull.

"I like his head," Mwembe said.

That was life in Kikambala—slow-motion. I felt as if I'd entered the great heart of a whale whose every beat lasted a lifetime and in between I could find all the parts of myself and stitch them together before jumping back on my itinerary. Nothing happened there, but Mwembe taught me to breathe one breath at a time, not to break into a run, but to lift each foot and move with the grace of a beautiful child.

※

I was always thirsty. We bought water at Ali's *duka*: eighty cents for a gallon. You filled your tin yourself from a spigot stuck in the ground. I didn't know if it was safe, so I drank the water only as coffee the first few days, but the coffee didn't quench my thirst. If I made the twenty-minute walk to the Cantina for a Coke, I was parched and sweaty by the time I got back.

One afternoon, Mwembe cut open an immature coconut and insisted that I drink all the juice inside. "Get a cup," I said. "We can share it."

"No, it is new for you."

I raised the rough skin to my lips and drained it. The juice was sweeter and richer than the watery stuff in mature coconuts and it slaked my terrible thirst. The flesh inside was like a jelly. We scooped it out with a spoon, ate it, and tossed the husk onto the ground.

---

22. Ibid.

※

Mwembe threw all our garbage on the ground in front of the door: banana peels, potato peeling, crusts of bread, soaked coconut flesh, fish bones, cabbage scraps, eggshells, mango and orange rinds—everything. The goats joined the monkeys and chickens in our rubbish heap to tidy up every morning. The goats ate all peelings except lemon; chickens loved tomatoes; nobody, not even the monkeys, ate the cabbage leaves; a goat carried off the leaves from the cassava plant that Mwembe cut so I would know what the plant looked like. The crows and chickens bickered over the coconut husk and picked it clean together.

One morning, five goats came galloping up, as if word had gone out that a banana peel had just been tossed. Banana peels were the goats' delicacy-of-choice. They usually grazed their way over, sniffing and biting at everything along the way, but those guys were on the run. They didn't stay long, looked mildly embarrassed at finding nothing to scavenge, and then galloped away.

It was chicken-mating season while I was there. The rooster chased the hens around ferociously. The hens even came squawking up on the porch, then they leapt down, circled through the trees, around the garbage, dove in the weeds, but the roosters were fast. After one particularly rowdy session, a bedraggled red hen returned on her own to make her nest in the dirt in front of me. She stirred and scratched in the dust for half an hour, her legs up and flying, then she rolled in the dirt, pecked at it, turning around and around, squatted and wiggled for a minute, then was up and pecking again. Next, she walked around the burn pile and had a go at a more promising site, same routine, same result, but she couldn't find comfort, couldn't drop the egg, couldn't stop trying.

※

The days were filled with repeated behavior. Things crashed from the sky all the time. I saw or heard seven or eight small explosions every day; usually it was a coconut or a whole palm frond—20 to 30 feet long—falling more than 50 feet to the ground. Limes and immature coconuts also fell, but with less fanfare. The continual crashing to the ground contributed to the fatalistic feel of the place, and the debris and garbage everywhere heightened the sense of living by rhythm and by chance. Let things lie until you need them; what will fall, will fall; God knows.

※

Mwembe sawed wood most mornings. Working hard, he would say. Although every time I went over to the tree he worked under, he was talking to somebody. I commented on his many interruptions.

He smiled happily. "These are my friends."

"Yes, but you are poor. You must work."

"I am working," he said. "Take my picture." He transformed himself from a gregarious kid in a fishnet tank top and white sailor's cap to a serious workman, intent on the job; his friend put a steadying hand on the board so I'd include him in the picture.

Later, I walked down to the beach. The tide was nearly at the line of the horizon, 300 hundred yards out. The deserted beach was beautiful as a postcard with flawless white sand and a line of coconut palms whispering in the wind, but I was uneasy being alone in so much space. I thought of the Peace Corps Volunteer twenty years earlier whose body was washed up and buried by the local people in an unmarked grave on a beach just like this one. Nobody knew he was missing until his up-country school called the Peace Corps office to complain that he hadn't been in the classroom for two days.

I'm not good in water alone, and it was a long way out there, so I lay on the sand in the shade, but that brought no comfort either. The continual wind kept the sand rolling along the beach, and I was coated with grit almost immediately.

※

Later, just before sunset, Njoroge and I walked down to the ocean again. "What was the first African country to get independence?" he asked. Njoroge was a natural teacher.

"Ghana," I said.

"No!" he shouted. "Everybody says Ghana, but it was Egypt, from the British in 1922. You must remember that Egypt is part of Africa."

"Of course," I said humbly. The tide was high and on its way out. We waded in a few feet; the water was uncomfortably warm.

"The Luo are our fiercest people," Njoroge said, a Kikuyu himself. "They are known for their *kali* temper." He waved to a group of girls sitting on the beach not far from where we were walking. "The Luo are also our most learned people."

We stopped to talk to the girls. There were five of them, lovely young Kenyan women, modestly dressed. After Njoroge introduced me, the most forthright girl looked me up and down with wide, sharp eyes. "Hello," she said in a voice that was not friendly. "Who is she?" she asked Njoroge in Swahili. "Why is she with you? Are you sleeping with her?" The girls didn't know I understood.

I shifted my weight back and forth in the sand. "The water is warm," I said, to change the subject. "Have you been in?"

"Give me money, miss," the girl said, then laughed and turned to Njoroge. "She is old," she said in Swahili.

We walked a half mile down the beach, then turned back. The girls were still there, some distance from us, when they spied two German women. They flocked up, smiling and curtsying. I heard the leader say. "*Jambo!* How are you liking Kenya?" The round-eyed hostility she had turned on me was hidden. They *jamboed* those old ladies for all they were worth.

That everybody thought I was Mwembe's and Njoroge's sugar mama took some getting used to. I went to the Whispering Palms bar alone one day to get something cold to drink and to sit in a chair. I'd developed a pinched nerve and could hardly support my own back sitting on the slab in front of the room. I'd been frequenting the Cantina, but the only other white people there were German men with money and sweet words for the young Kenyan women. The white men regarded me with the particular interest that the Kenyans did, whispering out of the side of their mouths while staring and laughing. I thought I could blend into the tourist crowd at the hotel.

When I entered the poolside bar, a waiter was placing a tray of beer and soft drinks on a table for a quartet of women near the door. A lone swimmer was doing a lazy backstroke up and down the pool, and an assortment of plump, middle-aged tourists were sunning themselves while wearing the barest suggestions of swimsuits. I took an empty table. It was pleasant; I was cool and relaxed under the shelter, happy to be anonymous for a moment, relieved to be sitting in a chair with a back.

"It is Mwembe's woman," somebody said in Swahili.

I looked up. Two waiters were leaning on their trays at the other end of the bar, talking about me. They made no attempt to lower their voices or serve me; one glanced at me just as I looked up. "She is cooking with Mwembe," he said.

I raised my chin to get their attention, to place my order, but both waiters stared past me. Finally, I got up, walked to the bar, and asked for a Coca-Cola. I took it back to my table, drank it quickly, and left. I never went back.

※

At eight o'clock in the morning, the heat had already left me limp on the slab in front of the room. Mwembe hovered before me. "I cannot finish the cupboard without more nails. I am going to Mombasa for nails."

"I thought Njoroge was bringing you nails yesterday." Njoroge went to Mombasa every other day to buy supplies for the Cantina, where he was employed for about a dollar a day.

"He did not find nails," Mwembe said. "There is a nail factory in Mombasa, but it is too hard to find them."

"Okay," I said and leaned back on my pad.

He gave me the key to the room but lingered anxiously.

"Don't worry," I said. "I will take care of everything."

He smiled with that straight line of perfect teeth and tucked his red shirt in his shorts—the shorts Maria sent that were too small for him. He wore them because they came from her. "Okay," he said. He was reluctant to leave me, conscious that the host should hover around his guest at all times.

When he returned hours later, he'd brought lunch: two strips of cassava, roasted and spread with *pilipili,* wrapped in leaves; one green mango, spread with *pilipili,* four small bananas; two hard-boiled eggs; one ripe mango.

"This is a delicious lunch," I said when he unwrapped the food. We were squatting in the dark room because it was cooler inside than outside in the middle of the day.

"You call it cassava in your country," he said.

"I have never seen cassava in my country."

"That is the English word. We call it . . . ," and he said the Swahili word.

"I have had the best food in Kenya here in your house." It was true; we ate beans cooked in coconut milk with tomatoes, potatoes, and onions; meat boiled with spinach; rice and fish with tomato sauce and *pilipili;* peas and dried corn cooked with tomatoes, potatoes, and onions.

He rocked back on his heels, pleased. "That is good," he said.

"Did you get the nails?"

"No, there are no nails. Just as Njoroge told me."

"That's impossible."

He shrugged. "There is a nail factory right in Mombasa, and I can buy no nails. If I buy one kilo, two kilos, maybe I can get nails, but for a poor man like me . . ." Mwembe was not one to complain. "Tell me about this mountain again."

I had told him about climbing Mount Kenya the week before I arrived in Kikambala. He had never heard of Mount Kenya, the second highest mountain in Africa after Kilimanjaro. He had never heard of Kilimanjaro.

"Where is that mountain?" he said.

I got out my map and showed him. He looked at the map for a long time, looked at Mombasa, Kikambala, the town where his parents lived. He traced the road to Nairobi; he had taken the train there with Maria and stayed at the Central YMCA; he spoke of that trip and the Central YMCA often. He pored over the map for half an hour in the dark room with a flashlight.

When I started to clean up from lunch, he jumped up to do it.

"No, I will wash the dishes."

I'd watched the other women wash, and I was ready to draw water from the well, find coconut debris for a scrubber, and do it myself. I took the dishes outside and sat on a small stool in the dirt to the side of the house; I didn't want Helen or the other women to see me because they'd laugh or, worse, they'd try to do it for me. Mwembe didn't care if I was clumsy; he was content to lie on the porch and look at the map; he would be equally content to let me lie on the porch while he cleaned up. Work was not work to him; it was part of life to be shared.

※

One night, Mwembe had a cold, or maybe the flu, and he and Njoroge came to me for *dawa*, medicine.

I unwrapped some Alka-Seltzer Cold Medicine—it was all I had. He gasped when he saw the big flat tablets.

"Don't worry," I said. "We put them in water, like this." I dropped them in a glass and both boys jumped like the tablets. The noise of the "zitzing" *dawa* was magnified in the small room lit by the flame of the lamp flickering against the wall.

"This is very good medicine," Mwembe said solemnly. His whole body had grown limp and sad. By contrast, Njoroge was hopping about like some insect, waiting to see what would happen when the tablets dissolved.

I gave the glass to Mwembe. "You must drink the whole thing for it to work." I was afraid he'd recoil at the taste or have some superstition against drinking such a strange concoction, but it was the only cold medicine I had.

He took it willingly and solemnly chugalugged it.

"Hey," Njoroge said, "I want to taste it."

Mwembe gave him the glass, with a third of it left.

Njoroge raised it in a toast and downed it like vodka.

"Hey," I said, punching him in the shoulder. "What did you do that for? It was medicine, *dawa*, for Mwembe. You're not sick."

Njoroge gave me the universal shrug. "It is nice medicine. I wanted to taste it."

I ranted about how Mwembe was cheated of the proper dosage, but neither of them was impressed. Mwembe didn't mind sharing with his friend Njoroge. I'm sure they wondered why I made such a big deal about common generosity. Of course, Mwembe would share anything he had with Njoroge. I stifled my urge to say, I know how your culture works, how unbelievably generous and gracious you are to one another, but sharing medicine is stupid; the sick one doesn't get a sufficient dosage and the healthy one . . . well, you know.

The next morning Mwembe arrived unsmiling again—still sick. "I cannot work today," he said.

I brushed off the mattress. "Lie down in here for the day. You'll feel better, get some sleep."

"No," he said, waving his fingers at me. "It is better to sit on the porch. If I go to bed, I am giving this sickness the chance to get all over me, to cover me." His fingers fluttered weakly across his body. "I must stay up and fight it."

"But it is germs that have made your body sick. You need rest to fight those germs, to make your body strong enough to kill them."

He smiled at me tolerantly and rolled his eyes at Njoroge. Nonsense, his look said. He stretched out on the cement slab when Njoroge left for the Cantina and was asleep in minutes.

There were no windows or ventilation in the room, so it was pitch black at night and stifling with the aromatic humidity of the boys' clothes dangling over my head. The room was lit by a single paraffin lamp until I went to sleep, then by the faint glow of the mosquito coil that burned under the bed. I imagined that the coil breathed poison into the narrow room, but I didn't care. It kept the mosquitoes off me, so I could lie naked on top of the sheet.

It was usually quiet, too. I heard only the faint sounds of the sleepers down the row of rooms, so I was startled awake by a pounding on the tin door one night. A man shouted, "Mwembe?" The padlock rattled in the loop. "Mwembe!" he shouted.

I lay quietly. I wasn't to open the door for any man.

"Let's go dancing," the man shouted in English and struck the door again. "Mwembe!"

I waited but said nothing. He wouldn't be speaking English if he really wanted Mwembe.

"Let's go to the disco at Whispering," he called.

I imagined that Helen and her babies were lying there, listening to this, and the mama of Tieno and her husband, and the old man at the end. I waited a long time before going back to sleep.

The next morning, Mwembe asked me if somebody had come in the night.

"Yes. It was quite late."

"It was this beach boy, this Gordon." He was clearly upset. "He shouldn't interrupt in the middle of the night or even early in the morning . . . you might be having a dream. He might be interrupting something really important. Nobody should interrupt a dream."

"It's okay," I said. "I wasn't dreaming."

"Let me tell you a story," he said. "There once was a man who was inventing the first computer. He worked and worked—for six long years, working very hard. He was very close to solving the problem, to getting it all finished. He had taken all his materials, notebook, his pens, papers, all his calculations, off in the bush, to work on it. His wife didn't know what he was doing every day, and she became very curious. So on this day, when he was so close, only two weeks, three weeks, from completing the project, the wife followed him to see what it was that he was doing all the time, and when she got close to him, she said, 'What are you doing?'

"He was so involved, so concentrated, he didn't say anything.

"Again, she said, 'What are you doing? What are you doing there with all that writing?'

"Again, he didn't say anything, didn't lift his head, and the third time she said, 'What are you doing? What are you doing?'

"At that, his head jerked up and he burst into tears and sobbed and sobbed, didn't stop crying. He got up and followed his wife home, and was still crying, still sobbing, into the house, and he cried all night, and it was only the next morning that he was able to stop crying and to explain to her that when she spoke to him she interrupted his thoughts, interrupted his dream. He lost the rest of what he was thinking about, and he would never find it.

"The wife started to cry because it would have been so much money, he would have been famous. Then she took all of his papers, all of his calculations to the university, to some scientists, to see if they could find the clues to what he had lost. The scientists took all his calculations, and they solved the problem. They were the ones who introduced the first computers to the world and got all the credit and all the money.'

"So," he said. "Do you see? You must let somebody finish a dream."

*

Ali, the *duka* owner, who sold water as well as matches and tinned foods, was the only man in the immediate neighborhood who was rich enough to have more than one room for his family. Ali's children stopped by our cement slab nearly every day. Mwembe always tipped our pot of food to them and invited them to eat; the girls laughed shyly and refused, but the little boy, Nasser, always scooped out a bite or two.

I stuttered in my infantile Swahili with Ali's wife when I bought something at the store; once she invited me in to see her house, with its six rooms radiating from a central courtyard.

I bought three rolls there one morning; Njoroge hadn't shown up for breakfast, but Mwembe was pumping the stove to heat water for coffee as I spread tinned margarine on the rolls.

"Did he talk to you?" Mwembe asked.

"Who?"

"That *duka* owner. Ali."

"No, I didn't see him. Why?"

Mwembe shook his head seriously, without the usual wide grin. "Yesterday, he take me in his house and ask me something."

"What did he ask you?"

"He ask me to give him two thousand shillings."

"That's crazy. What did you say?"

"I just laughed, but it is not good." He filled the coffeepot with water bought from Ali and put it on the stove. "It was very wrong for such a man to ask me for two thousand shillings. He is my father. I am young, he is old."

He rocked back on his haunches and looked at me. I could see that he was disturbed by this incident—he had waited a day to mention it. "It is very bad for him to ask me this, very bad. An old man can ask to borrow ten shillings, but never so much money from a boy like me."

The whole thing made me uneasy: Ali would never have asked Mwembe for money if it weren't for my presence; he must have assumed that I was rich and buying Mwembe's body or something. I tried to make a joke of the whole thing. "Maybe Ali is just a crazy man."

Mwembe clicked his tongue. "Maybe he wants to take my money to do witchcraft on me. He thinks he can take what is mine to hurt me." The water was boiling; he filled our cups and handed me the red one. It was too hot for me to drink, but he gulped half his down, obviously preoccupied with this strange request from the richest man in the village.

"Okay," he said and smiled at last. "I will try to become a man who might have two thousand shillings to lend. If the *duka* owner thinks it is possible, then maybe God will, too, and it will happen." He was glowing. "Yes, I shall become a man who has two thousand shillings to lend."

※

On my last night, we sat on the cement slab in the moonlight for a long time. Mwembe told me how happy he was to have me as a visitor, that it was good to have visitors, that any kind of visitor was wonderful because he wanted to be the sort of person people visit.

"I am lucky because I always have many visitors," he said. "Not just tourists, but other boys in the village always come to my house in the evening to talk. I like that."

He spoke modestly, to convince me how glad he was that I had come to him. He told of helping the mother of a friend to buy a little flour from time to time; he was pleased to be asked. "I feel lucky that there is no problem in my personality so that people come to me."

"By tomorrow, when you are gone," he said, "it will be very lonely around here. It will seem that the room is too big." He laughed, knowing that the room was very small, but he said it again. "The room will be too big for me and Njoroge when you are gone. We will never forget you."

I could only stammer out a few words—I would never forget them, they had been so unexpectedly, extravagantly kind.

The next morning, they stood at the edge of the village and waved goodbye as I trudged down the road with my duffel on my back. I stopped once and looked back at the two of them standing there and thought of taking one last picture, but I didn't do it. The picture could never show enough—two young men lifting their hands to welcome me, opening their room to me, calling to me from the path to share their food, showing me how to breathe one breath at a time, and how to move with the grace of a beautiful child.

Brighter Futures

A place doesn't tug at you the way a child does—the last words in the journal I kept during my month as a volunteer at Brighter Futures Children's Home, in Bistechap, a village of seventy-nine households southeast of Kathmandu, Nepal. The valley was beautiful, the village exquisite. The wheat was ready for harvest when I arrived, golden stalks swaying in the breeze across a vast valley and up terraced hills, nearly to the giant golden Shanti Ban Buddha who shed his universal light on us during the day and who glowed through the star-filled nights. I heard bells in the morning welcoming the spirits in every household, smelled incense burning, saw the mist lifting, and the green day unfolding. In the distance, women in bright red, yellow, and purple saris harvested the wheat, cutting it with a scythe, piling it on their backs, huge sheaves twice their size, walking the narrow paths home where they spent the next several days beating the stalks on the ground, separating the wheat from the chaff. By the time I left, the shorn wheat fields had been tilled with short-handled hoes by hand, and seeded with rice, the paddies now brilliant green rectangles up and down the valley. It was stunning.

So the place was beautiful, but it is the fourteen children, ages six to sixteen, nine boys, five girls whom I think about every day, who taught me the power of human connection and the sweetness of simple things, a story, making music, picking wild berries along the path, skipping rope, talking, making a joke, laughing together. I knew about such pleasures of course, but living with these children who had lost their families and who had few material possessions, but who greeted each day with joy and curiosity reinforced my belief in basic human goodness and in the responsibility we all share for the health and well-being of each other.

They taught me concrete things too such as *don't waste food*. We ate *dal bhaat* twice a day, a huge mound of rice—*bhaat*—on a wide metal plate, seasoned with a thin lentil—*dal*—soup, and garnished with a spoonful of curried vegetable—potato, okra, cauliflower—the vegetable being the only variation day to day—prepared by Sita Didi. (*Didi* means big sister; I was Kathleen Didi.) The boys sat in one row on the floor, the girls in a row perpendicular to them, I faced the boys and Sita Didi sat to my right surrounded by our fifteen plates, doling out the *dal bhaat*. When the plates were ready, each person picked up their own, in order, handicapped children first, then the youngest to the oldest. The *dal bhaat* was delicious but sitting cross-legged on the floor hunched over my plate, eating hot rice and thin soup with the fingers of my right hand left an embarrassing halo of *dal* to mark my place on the floor. As the children finished eating, they took their cup and plate to the water spigot outside, washed each and set them on a rack to air dry. I watched them closely to know what to do, but the first time I washed up, I rinsed a bit of rice off my plate. "No, no!" seven-year-old Udai shouted. "You are wasting. Give it to the chickens."

I was ashamed. At the next meal, Udai demanded to see my plate before I cleaned it, then wouldn't let me approach the spigot until I had pinched the last grain of rice from my plate and had drunk the last drop of liquid.

"You are the *dal bhaat* police," I complained. He was delighted to be the *dal bhaat* police and from then on, lay in wait for me after every meal.

Udai, aka the dal bhaat police.

Life there was simple. Days unfolded predictably with a rooster alert at 4:00 a.m., children stirring at 5:00 a.m., everybody up by 5:30 a.m. performing their morning ablutions at the cold water tap as the tinkle of bells rippled through the valley. By 6:30 a.m., the farmer's boy had delivered the milk and Sita Didi was boiling it for the children. Then morning chores: everybody swept their area, polished their shoes, somebody got the newspaper from the tea shop and children crowded around to read it; others lined up to get their vitamins or ear drops or antiseptic on their nose piercing. We ate *dal bhaat* at 8:00 a.m., then there was a flurry of washing dishes, brushing teeth, getting dressed for school, primping in front of the mirror, filling their water bottles with boiled water, picking up the tin with their snack from Sita Didi, organizing their backpacks, and by 9 a.m. we were all walking up the steep, muddy hill to wait for the school bus.

Tell us a story. Every morning the same request as we walked up the hill, the older children as insistent as the younger: *Tell us Sleeping Beauty, no, Robin Hood. We had Robin Hood yesterday, do Puss 'n Boots, no, please Robin Hood. You promised.* I told a lot of stories that month, over and over, their eyes round when the ogre or witch or the evil Sheriff of Nottingham appeared, eyes shining when the prince finally showed up and at the end, when I paused, everybody chorused *"and they lived happily ever after."*

Which is my most fervent wish for these children, that they live happily ever after. Thanks to Emma Cahilog-Rahman, the Executive Director and Founder of Volunteer Service in Nepal (VSN), the children have an excellent chance of doing just that. When Emma took a holiday from her position as a university professor of philosophy in the Philippines to trek in Nepal, she fell in love, not only with the beauty of that rugged country but with the man who became her husband. Soon after her marriage, she determined "to do something for Nepal."

New Zealander Colin Salisbury was just then organizing Global Volunteer Network (GVN) and was looking for a local partner in Nepal. He met Emma at a time when she realized that helping children was the most pressing need. The ongoing Maoist insurrection had left countless orphans in the remote villages and many other families, fearing for their children's well-being, had sent them to one of the numerous children's homes that were springing up in the relative safety of the Kathmandu Valley. When ten volunteers from New Zealand arrived in 2003, it was these children that they and Emma set out to help.

The challenges were enormous. Many, not all, of the orphanages those first volunteers worked in were run by owners who took advantage of the generosity of donors and the fears of poor parents, most of whom paid relatively large sums to place their children. Emma drew up many contracts with the owners, to specify how they would use the resources VSN provided and time after time the contract was broken. When they raised money to provide a water filter for a home, the owner moved it into his quarters and the children had no clean water. A facility was renovated by VSN so children who had been sleeping outside could sleep inside and the owner moved his family into the space, and the children continued to sleep outside. Early on it was clear that VSN needed to operate their own children's homes in order to ensure adequate care.

Five years later, VSN was operating two children's homes, serving fifty-one children, in addition to providing volunteers to other children's homes when feasible or to teach in government schools. Emma's mantra is sustainability. VSN must have control over the homes so they can ensure consistent care for the children, and the homes must function well even if there are few volunteers. As GVN has expanded their program—they now send volunteers to twenty-six countries (including the United States)—fewer volunteers come to Nepal. "Everything we do must be sustainable," Emma says.

As part of our volunteer orientation, we toured both of VSN's homes plus another run by a private owner. The contrast was startling and disturbing. In the two VSN homes, the children were happy, clean and well-fed, kind to each other, full of curiosity about us; the homes were bright, attractive, simple, but clean, and those children have a future, a bright future. VSN sends them to a private school where the language of instruction is English and is committed to supporting them through college. These children will be well prepared to do something for Nepal.

At the other owner-run home, there were no adults present the day we showed up, and the fifty children housed there were unkempt. Several seemed listless; others were obviously glad to see us and followed us about as we looked into their dim rooms; four little boys, six or seven years old, were asleep on the floor in one room; another boy, about seven, was sitting alone, tugging at his ear. When we looked closer, it was clear that he had a severe ear infection—swollen and painful to the touch. One member of our group had some Tylenol which the VSN staff person cut into thirds, gave one to the child, wrapped the other two in a scrap of paper, and told him to take one at bedtime and one the next morning. She asked one of the older boys to keep an eye on him and then we left, uneasy and heartsick.

The focus now in such homes is on the health of the children; a health volunteer stops in regularly to do a health checkup including taking children who are ill to a clinic, but VSN is no longer willing to provide anything beyond basic medical care because they can't guarantee that their efforts will help the children. While I was there, the manager of another poorly run home said he no longer wanted to work with VSN. When the volunteer told the children she had to leave, they said, "Now we won't have enough to eat again."

The children at Brighter Futures always had enough to eat. At my last meal there, Sita Didi added a fried egg and French-fried potatoes (chips) to my *dal bhaat*—an unimaginable treat. (I first heard about it from the children—*Didi has made chips for you! Just for me? Yes.*) It sounds silly, but when I saw the chips and egg on my plate, *only* my plate, it brought tears to my eyes. The children got quiet, watching me, wondering what was going to happen as I sat cross-legged and choked up before my plate of *dal bhaat* and chips. I took a deep breath, picked up a chip, nodded my thanks to Sita Didi, and we all began to eat.

❋

When I came home, my grandchildren saw my pictures and listened to my stories. "Did you tell them about us?" one asked. VSN keeps meticulous records on the children, including family history: "parents killed by Maoists," "no known family," "living parents, no contact," "father dead, mother unable to cope," "parents killed," "no parents." So yes, I did tell them about my grandchildren, but not too much. The contrast was too great. Still, my granddaughter's question lingered because she and those children are deeply connected and dependent on each other.

There is a truism in teaching that says it is the teacher who learns the most; the corollary is true for volunteers. It is the one who volunteers, who tries to give, who receives the most. Those children were glad to know me, they loved my stories, they learned to knit and finger crochet because I was there, but right now there is another volunteer who is loving them, helping them, teaching them karate or singing songs with them, maybe even somebody who can tell a good Robin Hood story. I was part of their lives for one month, a tiny footnote as their story moves forward. They will forget me, but I won't forget them because they showed me the beauty of the human spirit, they reminded me that joy and curiosity are fundamental human qualities, that it is never about what you have but who you are, and that all children are our children.

Emma is now looking for volunteer opportunities for the children. "They have so much," she said. "Ample food, health care, a good education. We can't make it too easy for them. They must give back too." How lucky they are to have a chance to volunteer because it is the volunteer who benefits the most. I know.

Second Time Around

I joined the Peace Corps at twenty-one because I was restless for adventure and after two years in Ethiopia, discovered that true adventure lies in the relationships and routines of daily life. I was delighted to live in a tiny mud house with a tin roof, thought the sound of roosters in the morning and the whoop of the hyenas at night exotic, learned to prefer fiery food that made me sweat and cry, but the surprise was my students. I fell in love with them—seventy-five kids in an unlit classroom with mud walls and a tin roof, seventy-five kids, many who walked an hour or more to get to school, kids whose parents I never met, whose fourth or fifth language was English. They were my adventure.

After two years, I came home, married, and embarked on that other adventure, raising children and living on a tree-lined street in a Minneapolis neighborhood. But when we entered that limbo state some call retirement, Chuck and I got restless again and in 2016, we took a job teaching at Zhejiang College of Media and Communications in Hangzhou, China. We knew it would be interesting, knew we would learn more than we would teach, knew it would be great, but, at first, we didn't recognize this journey as a second chance.

There is something sweet about a second time around, a second taste, a familiar experience cloaked in new clothes. You are able to savor the taste, to breathe in the pleasure more deeply, to take in the sweetness with all your senses. We found it doing what we had done more than forty years earlier—teaching young people in an ancient country full of challenges, young people who were eager and optimistic about their future and who were also deeply aware of the enormous challenges their beloved country faces. In Ethiopia, the challenges were political first, then economic—who would succeed Haile Selassie; how would land reform be achieved? In China, it all starts with demographics—how to support a population of 1.4 billion people. As one student wrote, quoting an economist: "If we put the Chinese population in the richest country—America—America can't afford it either."

We were nervous that first Monday morning, unsure of who would be waiting for us and what they would expect. We both arrived twenty minutes early and found the students all there, three to a desk, in their jackets, hats, and mittens, warming their hands on bottles of hot water or tea. We introduced ourselves and invited them to do the same, in writing and in English, so we could get their English names for our class list and learn a little bit about each of them: name, hometown, interests and hobbies, hopes for the class. They came from all over China—as close as downtown Hangzhou, as far away as Inner Mongolia, but, incredibly, they all said they came from the most beautiful city in China, a city that is famous for . . . something . . . and they felt lucky to come from such a wonderful place. We were charmed by their lack of cynicism, their enthusiasm for their origins, and their deep admiration for their parents.

I taught writing and the reward for reading 240 essays every week was the insight I was given into the lives and worries of the students. Our twenty-year-old students with their deep attachment to their families and their physical connection to each other—always walking arm in arm, girls with girls, boys with boys—seemed younger than their twenty years, innocent, but they were not naive. When they wrote about the serious issues China faces, they were fully aware that these problems are their problems. They were the first generation of the one-child policy, and they believed in that policy, yet they wondered how they would care for their parents and grandparents without the help of siblings. According to a China TV news report, 75 percent of the average family's income goes toward education. After the government announced that education in rural areas would be compulsory and free through junior school (9th grade), one student wrote, "Our country's future depends on the next generation with good knowledge. How can we build our country with the junior school level?"

We were the oldest people on campus—the average retirement age in China is fifty for women, fifty-five for men—but the students treated us as peers, as fascinating people with something to offer them. They wanted to talk about everything. The movie *Brokeback Mountain* was much on their minds. They also wanted to know what we ate, what we thought about Japan, if children took care of their aging parents in the United States, if we fell in love at first sight, how we disciplined our children, what we thought of Jane Austen, if we watched *Desperate Housewives*, and why we came to China.

※

Our sense of wonder was rekindled by the simplicity of our life there. We lived in a small apartment on campus, walked or rode our one-speed bicycles everywhere, bought food daily, worked hard, made friends, took the crowded bus into Hangzhou on the weekends to walk along West Lake or drink tea (or coffee—yes, there was a Starbucks). We were glad not to own a car, and when students asked if we knew how to drive, we admitted that we could, but didn't mention the two cars in our garage in Minneapolis.

Doing without—no car, few clothes—was easier than slowing down. Colleagues talked about spending the day, the whole day, relaxing at a tea house. We tried, but couldn't figure out what you were supposed to do all day at a tea house. At every establishment we visited, the server brought us each a tall glass half full of tea leaves and filled to the brim with hot water then left a tall, pink thermos next to my chair.

No spoon to push the leaves down, no sugar, no lemon. If we tried to drink too soon, we burned our fingers on the glass and got a mouthful of tea leaves, so we had to wait for the leaves to sink. Even so, we were never able to last more than thirty minutes in such an establishment. We drank our tea, sometimes refilled the glass once from the thermos, and left.

It was a young teacher in our department who taught me how to drink tea. Kevin—I never knew his real name, his Chinese name—spoke beautiful English but wanted to sound like a native and asked me to help him with his intonation, so we practiced rising and falling inflections for a couple of hours a week. For our last meeting, he invited me to go to Qing Teng Tea House, the most famous in Hangzhou. It was obviously several steps above the tea establishments Chuck and I had frequented, and expensive—sixty yuan for a cup of tea. "We must have Hangzhou's most famous tea, Dragon Well tea," Kevin said.

The tea came in two tiny white china cups, no handles, but with lids and saucers. After a few minutes, I lifted my lid to drink. "No," Kevin said. "You don't drink the first or second water. The leaves are dirty." He lifted his cup and, using the lid as a shield, poured the water into the tall ceramic bowl on the table. (I'd thought it was a vase.) I did the same, and then he took the teapot of hot water that was on a small brazier near our chairs and refilled our cups. "Do you know what the lid is for?" he asked. Well, that was obvious—to keep the tea hot. He smiled, picked up his cup between two fingers and his thumb, raised the lid slightly, and breathed in the aroma of the tea. "The lid holds the flavor, so you take it in just as you sip the tea. Like fine wine," he said. "The bouquet."

Ah.

There was a tray on the table that we took to an adjoining room where there were two long buffet tables with hot and cold delicacies: spring rolls, soups, meats, fruits, tarts. Kevin filled the tray. "You must try this and this and this." Each was more delicate and wonderful than the one before and every time I said I liked something, he went back for more. After an hour or so, the server appeared to put a bowl of several kinds of fruit on our table, to refill our tea pot with hot water, and to rekindle the fire under the brazier.

Kevin had just bought a book of essays by Washington Irving, so we talked about Irving's place in American literature and "The Legend of Sleepy Hollow."

"What about Whitman?" he said. We also talked about the Hangzhou housing market and whether he should buy the apartment he was looking at near West Lake, half the size of his current apartment, but the location was tugging at him; and whether or not the teachers at our school cared about the students or were they more focused on the expectation to publish an article in a professional journal every year; and the Chinese aversion to bad news in any area of public life; and how you must know somebody in order to get a job; and many, many other things. When I looked at my watch, three hours had slipped by. That's how you can spend the day in a tea house. How simple. How lovely. How civilized.

He walked me back to my bus stop; I pushed on with the other commuters, clung to the strap as the old bus weaved around cars, bicycles, carts, and pedestrians for the hour-long ride back to Xiasha, the suburb where our college was. It was the last week of the semester and I didn't have to peer out the windows to know that the boulevard was lined with flowers, that the streets were crowded with people, that there was a woman on a bicycle with two children and the day's groceries, that a man was riding a bike one-handed with a load of lumber in the other hand, that the musical sound on the bus was somebody's mobile phone, that there were street signs I'd never learned to read, that there was row after row of small shops selling everything, that I was in China—China, one of the great civilizations of the world. China where people have suffered unimaginable indignities. China where there is so much hope and suspicion and life. It was hard not to wonder how I got so lucky.

An Ethiopian friend once told us that two years is so short in the life of a country, that what we could hope to achieve as Peace Corps Volunteers was fleeting, a tiny wave in an enormous whirlpool. He was right, of course. Five months teaching in a country with an 8,000 year history is even less, but for us it was a second chance. A second chance to fall in love with students, to be awed by how deeply connected each of us is on this planet, a chance to see ourselves as others see us, to be shaken out of our daily routine so we can see the power and the beauty of every day, of daily life, wherever we are.

During those two years in Ethiopia, I visited every province, saw the Blue Nile and the castles at Gondar, went to Lalibela, but what I remember and what I miss is my little mud house on a dirt road, the family across the way, the little girl who danced in the street, the students, especially the students. It was the same in China. I walked on the Great Wall, saw the terra-cotta warriors, floated through the three gorges down the Yangtse River, saw the lotus raise its huge and holy head at West Lake, but what I remember and what I miss are the people we knew, the students and young teachers who are the hope for the future. Fifty years earlier, I loved my students because it was impossible not to, but I was young too, and I didn't know how beautiful we all were. This time around I knew.

ONE MORE THING. We did this together, Chuck and I. We met in Ethiopia, but didn't live in the same town and in thirty-eight years of marriage never had the same job, or taught the same kids, or were irate at the same mindless bureaucracy. But in Hangzhou we understood what each other's day was like. We were colleagues as well as lifelong partners. I loved the sight of him coming up the sidewalk after class, notebook and papers in hand, looking professorial or sitting surrounded by "his" kids in the library. It was a gift, this second time around, to see each other in new light, to teach in China, to be amazed together.

Encounters

✼

Memorable encounters can happen anywhere, in the woods, at the school where you work, on a journey to a familiar place. These gifts, these unexpected meetings with a child, or an old friend, a place you loved and revisit, a place you never thought you'd be, or even an encounter with an insect can't be planned for or even anticipated. They are the gifts of being present and alive in this amazing world.

Dragonflies

Chuck and I were present at a gathering of dragonflies one summer, sitting on a rock overlooking Lake Agnes in the Minnesota Boundary Waters. It was that peaceful hour before sunset, just the two of us, happy to be there, not another person for miles. We'd had a great dinner, the dishes were washed, the food pack was hanging from a tree, the Deet was working and the black flies had momentarily forgotten our exact location. The loon was still in place in the middle of the lake, and the painted turtle had just crawled 6 inches up on the rock to see if we were still there.

Then, a dragon fly floated by.

We straightened up to get a better look, commented on the deep green of its body. Another dragonfly motored over, more helicopter than insect, up, down, dart forward, hard left, drop down.

Then another came and another . . . and another. Soon there were hundreds of dragon flies, thousands of dragon flies, millions and billions and trillions of dragon flies.

For more than an hour they swarmed above us, always in motion, the whir of their wings offering background noise to the quiet of the evening. It was magical. We had a warm rock underneath us, the still lake before us, and a swarm of dragonflies buzzing overhead. The only interruption was the change in sound when one dragonfly collided with another. Perhaps it was a dance or a game of dodge'em or a great spiral swirl that their biology insisted they take part in. After an hour or so one bound off, and then another, and another, and another. There were fewer of them, then very few, then two or three, then they were all gone, their disappearance as mysterious and as miraculous as their arrival.

I couldn't help but think about the generous, abundant universe displayed by all that frenetic beauty. The shimmering water around us—so much of it—the warm rock beneath us—so large and solid—the dependable procession of ducks, loons, flies, and mosquitoes, and all those luminescent dragon flies.

We live amid generosity and abundance every moment of our lives.

Hi, Robert Frost

Josie and Lauren, third graders, asked to interview me about Robert Frost because their teacher told them I had known Robert Frost.

No, I told them, I didn't know Frost, but I did hear him read in person.

Good enough, they said. They wanted me as a source for a report they were writing, so we agreed to meet.

※

When I heard Frost read in 1962, I was thrilled at the prospect of seeing a live poet, a famous poet, in person. I arrived early and positioned myself in the sixth row, center. The venerable old man with a shock of white hair and gravelly voice looked and sounded exactly as I imagined a poet would: cerebral, full-throated, ethereal, as if he had a foot in our world—Agnes Scott College, Decatur, Georgia—and a foot in the world of verse and imagination. Twenty minutes into the reading, he said he couldn't see to read, pushed the book aside, and declaimed from memory for the rest of the evening. I was spellbound.

So I never knew Robert Frost, but perhaps I could convey some of that magic to Josie and Lauren. I found my autographed copy of *You*

Come Too: Favorite Poems for Young Readers, downloaded recordings of him reading on my laptop, and met them at their school.

※

The girls were well prepared.

"How old was Robert Frost when you met him?"

I reminded them that I was an audience member, which is different from meeting him.

"But did you see him?"

"Oh, yes. I saw him."

"And he saw you?"

Well, yes, I wanted to think that I was seen by Robert Frost, right there in the sixth row, center. "Yes, he saw me."

"Did you say 'hi?'"

How could I answer that? Would I have been so rude not to say "hi" to the great poet? What would Josie and Lauren think? I didn't want to lie directly, so I nodded.

"And did he say 'hi' back to you?"

Now Frost's reputation was on the line. I'm sure he would have said "hi," to me if I had said "hi" to him, so I said, yes, he had said "hi" to me, and then I did what interviewees do when the questions are uncomfortable: I changed the subject. "What poems by Robert Frost have *you* read?"

Josie was on to my takeover attempt. "I have more questions," she said. "What was Robert Frost's favorite color?"

I admitted I didn't know and tried again to take control. "What do *you* think?"

"Red," Lauren said, and Josie immediately agreed.

Red sounded so wrong that I couldn't help but argue. "What about green or even brown? Maybe white."

They heard me out but wrote red in their notebooks. Next question. "What was Robert Frost's favorite food?"

I should have said I didn't know, but these girls had a report to write. I invoked the times—long ago; the terrain—a farm rich in chickens and potatoes. I surmised that his favorite food could have been potatoes or carrots, perhaps tomatoes, then stopped when I realized they were writing down my every word. "We don't really know, do we?" I said.

They wrote that down too.

I tried again to take charge and pulled out my laptop with the recordings of Frost reading. They listened politely, then were quite excited when I suggested they get a flash drive to transfer the recording to their classroom computer. After they successfully downloaded Frost, it turned out they had poetic curiosity beyond Frost. Had I known Rudyard Kipling? Did I have him on my computer? No. What about Emily Dickinson? No. William Shakespeare? No.

Aware that I was disappointing them with every answer and still thinking I could control the direction of the interview, I suggested that they memorize one of Frost's poems.

"Good idea," Josie said politely. "What have you memorized?"

I mumbled, "Stopping by Woods on a Snowy Evening" and hoped she wouldn't ask for proof.

She wrote it down and went to the next question. "What did Robert Frost teach?"

"I'm not sure he was a teacher," I said.

I must have sounded evasive, because Lauren followed up immediately. "But if he *was* a teacher," she said, "what would he teach?"

Skewered again. "He would have taught at the college level," I said.

She wrote it down.

In spite of her disappointment that I hadn't said hi to Dickinson or Shakespeare, Josie tried another tact. "Do you know any other poets?"

"Yes!" I said, relieved to tell the truth at last. "I do know other poets, poets who live right here in our city."

Their pleasure was obvious. They wanted the names, with correct spelling, of every poet I have ever said "hi" to. I felt better too. As I spelled out the names of poets I knew, I took on a little of the reflected magic of the poet, that inspired being who lives in our world, but whose language and rhythm transport us to another world. I hadn't been able to verify Robert Frost's favorite color or food, but I had let them in on the wonderful news that poets still live among us, and that they too might have the chance to say "hi" to a poet any day now. Josie and Lauren, at eight, are at that delicious age of devouring the printed word, of reading everything they see, and of being awestruck by poets.

And they have mastered the art of the interview.

Return

We returned to Ethiopia in 1997 to visit a student of Chuck's in Addis Ababa and to go to Dilla in southern Ethiopia where I had taught . . . and found change, dramatic change after thirty years of tumultuous upheaval in the beloved country.

Dilla

I knew my students wouldn't be waiting for me in Dilla; they were middle-aged now, or dead. It was the educated who were assassinated during the red terror after I left Ethiopia, after the coup, after Haile Selassie was deposed, and the "cleansing" of the new Marxist regime began. We were told that every family lost somebody, but maybe my students were too young or too far from Addis Ababa to be noticed. I knew I wouldn't find them, but after thirty years, I had to go to Dilla to see the school and my house and to eat at Amare's bar and to walk to Andida.

Chuck and I took the bus, still a ten-hour ride from Addis. I waited for the panoramic view you get of the town as the bus rolls down the switchbacks from the ridge at Kabado to Dilla, low at 5500 feet, waited to see the four dirt roads lined with whitewashed mud houses, the bus park on First Street, my house and the school on Fourth Street, and the wild green mountains beyond. The first time I got off a bus in Dilla, I didn't know where to go, so I asked a boy at the bus park where the Peace Corps lived and he took me to what would be my house. In those days, every boy was eager to walk with you or help you and knew just where to go. But I knew Dilla now—we wouldn't need a guide.

Suddenly, we were there, but without the dramatic descent or view of the town I'd waited for. The main road had shifted, the four streets were many streets, the population had tripled, and the town was now dominated by an enormous mosque at one end and a massive Coptic church at the other. Nothing was familiar. We walked every street, but I couldn't find the post office or Amare's bar where I had eaten lunch every day or even the house I'd lived in. We couldn't find Atse Dawit School where I'd taught sixth grade English and seventh and eighth grade math. So I did need a guide after all. We asked a boy, two boys, to help us.

"You looking for the high school?"

"There's a high school! No, not the high school. Atse Dawit School."

"Our school, Madam."

They were brothers, Mulukan, thirteen, and Kibro, ten.

It was still there.

They led us to the long grassy path I'd walked up every day to the mud and stone building with the tin roof that was Atse Dawit School. The soccer field was still on the right, where I'd stood with 7A every morning to sing "Ethiopia Hoy;" the outhouses still swarmed with flies; the old building still badly needed whitewashing.

It was July, the doors were locked, but Mulukan and Kibro took us to every room, made sure we looked through every window. I pressed my hands and face against the window into 7A, my homeroom. It looked *exactly* the same: rough wooden desks meant to seat two, more often holding four, the scarred chalkboard, stained, crumbling walls, no lights, no pictures on the walls, no shelves for books, no books. That beautiful, ugly, barren room was proof that I didn't dream the whole thing, that I had once stood in that dim classroom, writing on the scratchy board, solving for x with seventy-five wide-eyed students as rain drummed on the tin roof.

For a moment, I was twenty-three again and the two radiant boys, Mulukan in his jeans and faded striped shirt and skinny Kibro in windowpane plaid shorts that hung to his knees were my favorite students reincarnated, eager to help, hungry to learn, promising to show us everything. What else did we want to see?

Andida. I wanted to go to Andida. Walking to Andida had been a destination, something to do in a place where there was nothing to do, a village smaller, poorer, more remote than Dilla, accessible only by foot, an hour's walk up the mountain. The rich rode horses; the poor and Peace Corps Volunteers walked.

It was market day in Dilla, so we passed a steady stream of people coming *down* the mountain as we climbed up, most toting bags of onions or giant *inset* leaves, that draught-resistant miracle plant that shades the tender coffee bush and provides the starch that is the staple of the local diet. Everybody stared at us, the women laughing behind their hands and the men offering a hand and calling us *ferengi*. The ruts were deeper than I remembered, there were more people on the path and more huts along the way. No rich men on horses, but a wild man on a rusty motor scooter bumped down the mountain, dodging ruts wider and deeper than the tires of his old machine.

As we crested the rise and neared the village, Mulukan asked if we wanted to see the church. I'd never seen a church in Andida. Maybe it was a grand, new structure like the impressive mosque in Dilla. Maybe there was an old one with the traditional courtyard and octagonal church building, the outer ring for women, the next for men, and the inner circle protecting the ark of the covenant. Maybe the church would be resplendent with ancient paintings of saints or angels. Thirty years earlier, on a walk to Andida, we had discovered ancient stellae in a patch of corn outside a hut . . . and felt we had uncovered Tut's tomb. Maybe a revelation awaited us. Yes, we wanted to see the church.

They led us off the road, through a eucalyptus forest, and then down a wide path lined by twelve-foot-high *inset* plants. Clutches of old men draped in white, leaning on their sticks, flanked the path. They nodded as we passed, as if they'd been waiting for us. We arrived at a squat mud building with a corrugated tin roof in the center of a broad clearing at the crest of the mountain. "Where is the church?" I said.

"Here," Mulukan said. He glowed as he pointed to the sagging shack. The door was locked. "Wait," he said.

Chuck and I stood at the edge of the clearing and stared down the mountain we had just climbed. The vegetation was deeply hued and abundant, giant *inset* against the pale eucalyptus, the *inset* so green and lush that it left an impression of plenty wherever it grew. Mulukan soon returned with a priest and a key to the church. We stood respectfully outside the door and peered in. Mulukan urged us to enter, but I couldn't. Women are never allowed inside the central area of a Coptic church, and this church only had the center, one room, with a printed picture of St. George on the far wall, a sagging table, a candle, one chair, a bit of cloth draped over the one window, a fly whisk hanging on a nail. It looked like an abandoned storeroom. There was nothing about this shack that said "church" except the pride in the faces of the two boys who knew we'd want to see it, and the reverence of the old priest who opened the door.

Beautiful, we said. Thank you.

✤

We went to the Andida market, but nobody was there because the market was in Dilla that day. Weekly use had so sculpted the earth of the Andida market that you could imagine the people there, selling, buying, arguing. Years of trading had carved a maze of trails that looked like some kind of natural formation of gullies and plateaus. The flat areas where women had sat on the ground before cloths piled with spices, flours, or beans were smooth and elevated above deep trenches carved by bare feet.

It is empty, Kibro said. He was disappointed for us. No, I said. It is okay. That spectral market showed me that thirty years had indeed passed, but during those years of deep trouble in that beloved country, people had grown *inset*, ground it, sold it, bought it, walked to market, walked back, carving their footprints deeper in the earth. It was good.

As they led the way back down the mountain, Kibro slipped his hand into Chuck's as if it were the most natural thing in the world, boy and man, hand in hand, to show us we were still connected, to show us why we'd come.

Kathleen with Mulukan and Kibro at Atse Dawit School

Teacher

Most people visiting a head of state don't look for the cheapest accommodations, but we were returning Peace Corps Volunteers and couldn't see ourselves staying in the old Ghion Hotel or, worse, taking shelter at the new Hilton in the suburbs of Addis Ababa. We wanted to be in the center of town, near the Piazza, where we could step out our door and see goats and beggars and holy men. The Baro Hotel was cheap—US$12 per night—and the lush vegetation recommended it. Cascading bougainvillea and the *hadar abebe* bush with its giant red flowers curtained the long narrow porch in front of the rooms. A bit claustrophobic but perfect for the president's teacher. The room was simple, two cots, one lamp that was too dim to read by, and a tiny bathroom with a leaky toilet that kept the floor damp and musky. The proprietor, an enthusiastic young man named Feleke, served us tea, advised us to put our money in his desk drawer so we wouldn't be robbed, and wanted to discuss land policy. I admired the luxuriant red flowers. "I will give you seeds for your country," Feleke said.

"It is too cold," I said.

"You can try," he said.

That's what people were doing everywhere—trying. A doe-eyed

girl scrubbed clothes at a washboard in the corner of the courtyard as we drank our tea. Just beyond, an old guy scrubbed a Land Rover. On the streets, in the Piazza, young children were begging or polishing shoes or selling gum. Only the young men seemed not to be trying; they stood on corners everywhere, talking, watching, laughing, uncomfortably idle. Many were missing limbs—the most recent casualties of the thirty-year war with Eritrea.

By the second day of our return to Ethiopia, we had slipped into life there, hand into glove, in spite of the lepers with their smooth, stubby fingers and the beggar with his legs so swollen with elephantiasis that he had to be dragged from corner to corner. We weren't oblivious to the suffering but were hopeful that there was more to the story. Ethiopia had survived a bloody coup, civil war, terror and counter-terror, starvation, and some good men now held the future of the country in their hands.

We had come to see one of those men, my husband's student, Dr. Negasso Gidada, the president of Ethiopia. In a letter to Chuck, President Negasso had said, "I sometimes think that the years of struggle up to 1991 and my present position are partly the result of your lessons and the discussions we then had . . . you have contributed a lot not only for my own life but for the development and processes of struggle of our country . . ."

We arrived on a Saturday; Chuck called on Monday to set up the appointment. The secretary was guarded at first, then recognized his name. "Oh, you are the President's teacher," she said. "I will call you back." She called an hour later to say we were to be at the National Palace at 10:00 a.m. on Wednesday, the National Palace that had been the residence of His Imperial Majesty, Haile Selassie I, when we were Peace Corps Volunteers. What business did we have in going to the National Palace?

For the next two days, we tried to be tourists, but the impending visit hung over us. We were nervous. We did visit the University Lab School where Chuck had taught twelfth-grade history to Negasso Gidada, a bright boy from the remote village of Dembi Dolo. Chuck's journal entry for April 15, 1967, reads, "Negasso arrived at my home late, just as the curfew was imposed, and had to spend the night there. He is troubled by this whole mess [His Majesty's response to student demonstrations], determined to stick it out with the rest of his fellow students, but worried." We visited Haile Selassie Secondary School where I taught my first year before transferring to Dilla. We walked by the houses we had lived in. We visited the national museum and saw casts of the bones of our tiny, common ancestor Lucy, called *Birkinesh* in Amharic, *she is wonderful*.

We were dressed and pacing by 9:00 am Wednesday morning. Feleke had arranged for the cab and by the shy gathering of neighborhood children, night watchmen, and young women who worked at the hotel, it was clear that everybody knew that the president's teacher was about to leave for the palace.

We arrived at the black iron gates too early, but the guards were expecting us and let us in, on foot, unescorted. The spacious grounds had wide paths, manicured lawns, and the air was fragrant with flowering mimosa and frangipani, but it was absolutely silent, not even a gardener in sight. We held hands and walked slowly toward the palace in the distance.

A soldier met us inside the foyer of the large sprawling house that was the palace, showed us to an anteroom, told us to sit on a narrow, overstuffed sofa, and left us. We were too early. We stared at huge, framed lithographs of hunting scenes, intricately carved tables, a mounted head of some kind of antelope, a large Oriental rug on the floor, silver trays, china figurines. Nothing Ethiopian—gifts to head of state, we decided. We wanted to browse, to look at everything more closely, but we couldn't move. We were in the palace of the president and had been told to sit, so we sat.

At exactly ten o'clock, we were escorted to President Negasso's office. He rushed around his desk to take Chuck's hand in both of his, to hold on to him, to welcome him after so many years. He was a gracious man, balding, bespectacled, in a double-breasted suit, gold and black tie, neat mustache, with a soft voice and unassuming manner, so happy to see Chuck and, he said later, a bit surprised to find himself in Haile Selassie's office. He had studied history and planned to devote his life to the history of the Oromo people, but like so many bright young Ethiopians was out of the country on scholarship during the coup of 1974 and couldn't return. In fact, he was alive *because* he was caught outside Ethiopia rather than inside. Most of the students Chuck asked about were dead, either ". . . executed by Mengistu [the leader of the coup] or [they] sacrificed their lives in the long struggle for democracy, peace, and development."

It was an emotional hour. So much had happened since they were teacher and student. They talked about the recent history of the beloved country, about their own children, and their hopes for the future. They did what good men everywhere do, which was to speak regretfully about the past and hopefully about the future. They had gifts—the teacher brought books for his student and the president offered his teacher a copy of the new constitution, asked him to comment on it, and also presented a leather book with stamps issued since the dictator was deposed.

When it was time to go, I asked if I could take their picture together. As they stood for the photo, President Negasso moved from Chuck's right to his left, thus positioning his teacher as He-Who-Stands-At-My-Right, the traditional position of honor. "I'll not soon forget that," Chuck wrote in his journal.

An hour later, we walked back through the manicured grounds, through the iron gates, on to the road, found a taxi, haggled for the fare, were silent on the drive back. It was too much to talk about in the back of a cab. And when we got to the Baro Hotel, where a woman was scrubbing the long porch in front of our room, where two men were arguing, where a boy with a rough wooden box offered to polish our shoes, we lingered in the street next to the profusion of red flowers from the *hadar abebe* to take it all in. Everybody was trying. It was wonderful.

Chuck with President Negasso Gidada

The Art of Walking

Art here is taken to mean knowledge realized in action.
—Rene Daumal, French poet

In my mid-fifties I had a longing to slow down, a longing that came over me with an urgency I couldn't ignore. I was seeking quiet, slowness, sanctuary. I wanted to move through my days at a human pace, walking, without a cell phone or a day planner, and I wanted there to be some purpose to it, some direction. I was also drawn to being part of something much, much larger than myself. I was drawn to pilgrimage. As a Unitarian Universalist, the idea of a pilgrimage—of calling myself a pilgrim—was foreign to me to say the least. But I believe that the quest, the search for meaning, for discovery, and, yes, for adventure, is fundamental to being human. And so Chuck and I became pilgrims—twice. In the year 2000, we followed the ancient pilgrimage route to Santiago, Spain, walking 500 miles and, five years later, we began in Le Puy-en-Velay, France, and walked 1,000 miles to Santiago.

Historically, a pilgrimage was ***a physical journey to a sacred place***, present in virtually every religion: Jews to Jerusalem, Muslims to Mecca, Buddhists to Tibet, Hindus to Benares. In the Middle Ages, there were three great pilgrimage destinations for Christians: to

Jerusalem, to Rome, and to Santiago de Compostela. Legend has it that after the death of Christ the disciples dispersed to different parts of the then known world, to spread the Gospel. St. James—*Sant Iago*—went to Spain, we are told, where he spent a couple of years evangelizing. He then returned to Jerusalem, but was beheaded by Herod shortly afterward, in the year 44, Common Era. Immediately following his martyrdom, his followers are said to have taken his body to Jaffa, on the coast, where a stone boat was miraculously waiting for them and they set off back to Spain. They landed, some 20 kilometers from what is now Santiago de Compostela,[23] after a journey, which is purported to have taken only a week, thereby providing proof of angelic assistance. Just as they arrived, they saw a man riding along the beach whose horse took fright, and then plunged into the sea. When they reemerged, both horse and rider were covered from head to foot in scallop shells. The body was then buried in a tomb on a hillside, along with, later on, two of his followers, and then forgotten for the next 750 years.

Early in the ninth century, Pelagius, a hermit living in that part of Spain, had a vision in which he saw a very large, bright star, surrounded by a ring of smaller ones, shining over a deserted spot in the hills. The matter was investigated and a tomb found there containing three bodies. They were immediately identified as those of St. James and two of his followers and when Alfonso II, King of the Asturias went there, he declared St. James the patron saint of Spain. He built a church and a small monastery over the tomb in the saint's honor, around which a town grew up. News of the discovery soon spread.

It was encouraged to do so, to promote the town as a pilgrimage center, attracting money to the area—an economic benefit—and by the monks of Cluny, who saw in it the opportunity to assist the Spanish church in their long struggle against the Moors—political benefit.[24]

---

23. Santiago de Compostela contains a Romanesque cathedral completed in 1211 that was built on what was said to be the tomb of Jesus' apostle St. James. This tomb, discovered in the 9th century, became the most important Christian pilgrimage site in Europe after Rome. From the Encyclopedia Britannica.

24. Raju, Alison. *The Way of St. James: Le Puy to Santiago, a Walker's Guide*. Milnthorpe, Cumbria: Cicerone Press, 1999.

Thus, two iconic images of St. James appeared: St. James the pilgrim, dressed simply in his pilgrim's hat and cloak with a staff and gourd for water, and St. James the Moor killer, *Sant Iago Matamoros*. This second image recalls Ramiro of Castile's victory over the Muslims at the Battle of Clavijo (ca. 844). Christian participants said they saw St. James riding with them, slaying the enemy on every side. Thus, an iconography developed in which the horseback saint raises his sword in the midst of the fray, with dead and dying Moors at his feet—religion entwined with politics—a force in the *reconquista* of Spain.

For most of the history of the pilgrimage, people left from their own doorstep and began walking. A network similar to that of a river system grew up. Think of small brooks that join together to make streams, the streams join to make rivers, the rivers join to make one mighty river that came to be known as the Camino Frances, the road from France. It is true today. We met people who literally stepped out their front door and began walking—from Germany, Switzerland, Holland, England, but most, as we did, went to one of the historic joining points—where brooks became streams—because there was a cathedral or a priest who would offer a place to sleep and a blessing for the road.

The first time we started in Roncesvalles, the first town on the Spanish side of the Pyranees. In 2005, we began in Le Puy-en-Velay, in France, because it was a traditional meeting place for many pilgrims in the Middle Ages and the Bishop of Le Puy was one of the first pilgrims in the year 951—and it is a 1,000 miles from Santiago. It would take us a while to get there.

Lao Tzu said, "The journey of a thousand miles begins with one step." That was the journey we were on.

On both occasions, there were forms to fill out, and we were interviewed by a local cleric—asked if our pilgrimage was religious, spiritual, cultural, or athletic. As Unitarian Universalists, we said it was spiritual, which was duly noted in our *credentiale*, the pilgrim passport that we had stamped each night, proof that we were pilgrims who had made the journey on foot, and were entitled to the *compostela*[25] when we reached Santiago.

We thought our pilgrimage began in Le Puy, but as we slowly walked across the continent I came to realize that the real beginning for us was at the cathedral at Chartres. We'd had an extra day in Paris, so we took the train to Chartres because it was close, we'd never been there and, as it turned out, knew little about the cathedral itself and why it is so famous . . . until we stepped in.

There in the nave of the great cathedral was the labyrinth, built into the stone floor at the end of the thirteenth century. Labyrinths were constructed as a substitute for an actual pilgrimage for people who couldn't get to Rome or Jerusalem or Santiago. The labyrinth in the Chartres cathedral came to be called the "Chemin de Jerusalem," the Road to Jerusalem. We didn't know any of this the day we were there, but we were moved by the size and beauty of the labyrinth and by the men and women walking it. We toured the church first to prepare ourselves, walked the length of the nave, the choir, and the ambulatory.

We looked at the great rose windows, stopped before each altar, absorbed the cool and the calm of the cathedral, speaking in hushed tones like the other tourists—dare I call them pilgrims—and finally arrived back at the labyrinth, ready to walk it, bold enough to walk it, even though we wouldn't be walkers with our hands clasped in prayer as some were, or with our hands held out, palms up in supplication, moving one or two steps a minute as others were. We watched to see how people did it. We saw that you could walk at whatever speed, you could pass others, you didn't talk, didn't make eye contact, you kept moving, however slowly, and you walked the whole thing. A labyrinth is not a maze—there is only one way like the Camino—and you follow that way. It took a while. We had to focus on the walking, on the turns that brought us very near the center for a few steps and then

---

25. The *compostela* is a document created in the ninth century to certify that a pilgrim has completed at least 100 kilometers of the pilgrimage to Santiago.

to the outer edge of the labyrinth. Gradually, the focus became the beauty and calm of the walking not the victory or relief of arrival at the center.

We did arrive, however, with others there in the middle—fellow pilgrims. We milled about and looked about and finally we left, one by one, changed. Chuck and I sat on a bench outside the cathedral for a long while—people watching, glad to be there—and then we took the train back to Paris and left for Le Puy-en-Velay the next day to begin our pilgrimage, the *Chemin de Saint-Jacques*, the *Camino de Santiago*, the way of St. James.

We began our first day with the pilgrim's mass in the Cathedral at Le Puy—with more than fifty other pilgrims. The priest gathered us together after the mass, to bless us. He asked us each to say where we were from and how far we were going—all the way to Santiago, or an *étape*, a stage. We were Swiss, French, German, Norwegian, Belgian, Czech, Brazilian, English, French-Canadian, and two of us, Americans. He gave us each a small medal of St. Mary and sent us on our way. We were to be blessed many times in the next fifty-eight days, both formally by priests in churches and informally by the many angels who crossed our path.

That first morning—every morning—was stunningly beautiful. Most days we rose before dawn and were on the road between 6 and 6:30 a.m., walking on high plateaus, down plunging gorges, along country lanes, through shadowy forests, hamlets, and villages and every morning we said to each other, "Isn't this amazing? Have you ever seen such light?"

Conrad Rudolph says, "Experiences like these can happen anywhere. But they don't often happen with either the regularity or the strength that they did on the pilgrimage where every day is an adventure, potentially surreal, and where feelings so unconnected with modern existence become a part of everyday life."[26]

---

26. Rudolph, Conrad. *Pilgrimage to the End of the World: The Road to Santiago de Compostela.* The University of Chicago Press, 2004, p. 23.

Thousands of people do make this pilgrimage, but we walked alone most of the time, in others' footsteps, but just the two of us walking through field after field of wild flowers, across pastures held in by ancient, unmortared rock walls, with vistas of fields and farmhouse, sheep, cows, horses, in every direction; through sun-dappled eucalyptus forests; through waist high grass that left us soaked to the skin. We were enveloped by birdsong for hours. The sweetest voice of all was the cuckoo, far at the edge of the forest, every morning. We waited for it and didn't feel that the day had truly begun until we had heard, "Cuckoo, cuckoo." One of our rituals.

At night, we watched the swallows dip and dive around the church steeple, hundreds of them, dark shapes against the dusky sky. And often, in Spain, we watched the storks rearrange themselves in their nests atop church steeples.

More than once we met unaccompanied cows on the path. Somebody had opened the barn door and said, *Go, to the cows. Go to the pasture, you know the way,* and they did. And early one morning, on the Spanish side of the Pyrenees, we met twenty horses in the woods, walking alone, single file, on their way to their pasture. We stepped to the side of the path and they walked silently by, colts hurrying to cover their fear or shying away from us as they passed, mares and stallions trotting confidently by, heads held high as if we were only ghosts.

I've lived in the city most of my life. Encountering horses in the misty forest, cows and sheep grazing across my path, and being greeted by the cuckoo every morning was a mystical experience, was magical, was, finally, deeply spiritual. As Rudolph says, these things can happen anywhere, on any trip, but not with the frequency or the intensity of a two-month pilgrimage. And it doesn't happen if you travel by plane or car or even bicycle. You have to be on foot, moving slowly. As St. Augustine said, "*Solvitur ambulando.* It is solved by walking." I might add, it is also found by walking.

❉

One of the gifts of the Camino, the pilgrimage, is the other pilgrims—our family of the road. Who did we meet on the road to Santiago?

Susan put her flat up for sale, took the chunnel from England to France, the train to Saint-Jean-Pied-de-Port and began walking to Santiago in mid-June. Jean-Jacques had left his home in Egypt every year for the previous three to walk an *étape*, a stage of the road to Santiago. He walked for two weeks that summer and would walk the last étape the following summer.

Jan left his island off the coast of Norway to walk to Santiago, carrying a bracelet of beads that his church blessed him with for the trip. His wife, too ill to accompany him, urged him to go for them both and had a bracelet just like his at home. Each bead signified, he said: one for God, one for himself, one for the resurrection, another for the desert, one for agape—love, one for gratitude, one for happiness, another for silence, one for the night, and three for secrets.

Jean Pierre, an engineer by profession, carved a stick with his wife's and children's names on the top, a small scallop shell, and his calendar: a mark for every day. He said he was awed by how much poetry—*poesie*—that he found in himself on the Camino. Christine left her home in Sweden, her husband, and two twenty-something daughters, told them she was going to France to begin walking to Santiago. She had been ill for fifteen months before she left, sick with daily debilitating headaches, so exhausted she couldn't get out of bed most days, hospitalized for weeks. No diagnosis and nothing helped. She didn't know how long she would walk, how far she would get, but she was going.

They were our family of the road, our fellow pilgrims, the people we met.

There were many more of course: Lona and Lotte from Denmark, Pierre and Alain and Eliane, Dante, Gerhard, Doug, Stephan, Guy, Bartholomew (who we called the great communicator because he talked all the time), the Argentinean brothers Roberto and Pedro, Thierry,

Drew, Rob and Orling from the Dominican Republic—who said her name meant ray of light which described her perfectly.

Chuck called the Camino a monastic experience. There is a deep sense of community among pilgrims that is not dependent on language or profession or politics or wealth or nationality or, even, religion. There is communal living, ritualized, basic work and time for silence, time to be alone.

We stayed in *refugios*, refuges—usually renovated buildings, monasteries or seminaries, and once a tower—with large rooms with five to twenty bunk beds, blankets and pillows provided. Some were free—donation asked—most cost from three to twelve Euros per person, all reserved exclusively for pilgrims on foot, some took pilgrims on bicycles or horseback. On an average day we walked 15 or 16 miles, a distance you could travel in thirty minutes or less by car, even on narrow country roads. It was slow and often difficult. The path was rocky or slippery or narrow. Our packs were heavy. By 10:00 a.m. it was hot. By 11:00 a.m. every item of clothing was drenched with sweat; by noon we were exhausted and, most days, we didn't know exactly where we would sleep that night, if there would be a place for us, if it would be crowded, if there would be food available, if there would be hot water, if we would see anybody we knew. We usually stopped by 1:00 p.m., sometimes not until 2:00 or 3:00 p.m. depending on the day and the terrain and the availability of *refugios*.

When we found the *refugio*, we had our *credentiale* stamped, paid our fee, chose a bed, quickly pulled out our clean shorts and shirt, stood in line for the shower, washed our sweat-drenched clothes, hung them up, ate, and lay down to nap. Got up by 5:00 p.m. to see the church, shop for food, talk to others, write in our journal, take pictures. Same routine, same ritual every day.

The walking and the preparations to walk were our work, our monastic vocation. The time after showering and eating and napping were our rest times, our quiet times, were unimagined luxury because we had nothing to do during those hours, no phone calls to return, no presentations to prepare for, nothing to study, no meetings, no day planner or calendar in our backpack, nobody depending on us to do anything or be anything.

※

How did we know where to go? The way is marked by *balises* in France, red and white stripes on rocks, trees, signs, curbs, buildings, to indicate the GR 65—*grande route soisante-cinq*—and in Spain yellow arrows and scallop shells on rocks, trees, signs, curbs, and buildings. As with the labyrinth, you don't need a map or guide; you simply follow the way pointed out to you, the red and white *balises* or the yellow arrow.

※

Finding the path was particularly hard for Christine, the Swedish woman who was so ill. She was alone, disoriented, and could hardly speak to the other pilgrims in her first weeks. She had all those languages in her head—being Swedish, she is also fluent in English, French, and German—but she could hardly speak at the beginning, she said. It took her two days to walk what others did in one.

Everybody lost the path at least once. We did. We were walking through the small village of Pimbo in France one rainy morning, just after 7:30 a.m., happy to have walked so far so early, when a woman threw open her shutter, and leaned out the window to yell that we were going the wrong way. Her French was very fast and colloquial, but her message was clear—we were on the wrong path and if we would just turn and go the other way, back to the church, etc., etc., we would find our way. We weren't easily convinced—it was raining and the way we were headed looked good and was paved—but we finally did turn around and followed what we thought she had said. Two and a half hours later we found ourselves entering Pimbo for the second time that morning—we'd walked in a huge circle. The rain had stopped, and the direction was clear the second time we entered the village and so we headed out again, this time on the right path. It was a hard lesson—two and a half hours lost, an extra 10 kilometers walked. The red and white *balises* are there; the arrows point the way, but if you aren't attentive and looking, if you aren't present, you lose your way.

And there are the unexpected, sometimes awe inspiring, sights—the endless expanse of flowers on the Aubrac plateau, the artistic hand of a farmer in field after field. And sometimes unexpectedly tragic: We stopped for a break on a bench by a church in a little village one morning and were immediately approached by a woman with an urgent story. There had been an accident just an hour earlier on the corner across from where we were sitting—a boy killed by a car, a local child—so tragic, and she had to let us, complete strangers, know immediately. We held her hands and thanked her for the awful news.

Sometimes the unexpected was hilarious: The day after we were lost in Pimbo we were walking along a country road and, as I wrote in my journal, "The highlight of our morning was being wooed by a donkey. He came running toward us, through a field of cows and ran along the fence following us, braying loudly, galloping, begging us to take him with us, plaintive, insistent, persistent, as if we were the ones he had been waiting for all his life, and he couldn't believe we were walking by." I can still see the desperation in his eyes and his wide, white teeth as he brayed and brayed and brayed.

Then, a couple of weeks later, as we crested a hill in Spain, just before *Puente de San Nicolas*, an old man stood in the middle of the road leaning on his cane. We greeted him; he greeted us, said something about the bridge, and his house near it. I said, *no hablo espagnole*. He went on talking, explaining. As we started to go on, he took Chuck's hand, shook it, took mine, kissed me twice on the cheek. An hour or so later, we saw Alain and Eliane, and they had had the same treatment from the old man, including the two kisses for Eliane. And three years later, my friend Mary walked the same route—and she too met an old guy at that spot leaning on a cane who kissed her. So I guess he has his own mission or message for pilgrims—not all of it holy.

※

More than half of the people we met, both men and women, were walking alone, and there were more pilgrims than we expected. At first, I was disappointed, sorry not to be more special, more unique, but then I understood what an amazing, marvelous thing it is that so many people from so many places were taking two weeks, two months, three months to hoist up their pack and walk to Santiago.

In this fast paced, multitasking cell phone world, thousands of people of all ages, have put on the pack and the shell and the hat, taken their pilgrim's staff and headed for Santiago, walking across the continent at a snail's pace. Walking across the continent at a pace that *allows* them to notice the snails and the ants and the beetles, to hear the cuckoo, and to see the swallows dive.

We were transformed, not by our arrival in Santiago, but by setting out for Santiago, by getting up every day, swinging that pack to our shoulder and setting out, walking across another magnificent strip of this glorious planet, alone, with difficulty, with blistered feet, with shin splints, with aching knees, using the two feet God gave us, in the company of sheep and cows, barking dogs, and other pilgrims. As writer Phil Cousineau says, ". . . if the journey you have chosen is indeed a pilgrimage, a soulful journey, it will be rigorous. Ancient wisdom suggests if you aren't trembling as you approach the sacred, it isn't the real thing. The sacred, in its various guises as holy ground, art, or knowledge, evokes emotion *and* commotion."[27]

*

Christine told me her story one afternoon, sitting on the end of her bed in the *refugio* in Terradillos de los Templarios, on the meseta in Spain, hot, flat, dry land, on our forty-third day, her fifty-third day of walking. When she started walking, she was ill and disoriented and had no idea how far she would go, or how long, but after two weeks, her

---

27. Cousineau, Phil. *The Art of Pilgrimage: The Seeker's Guide to Making Travel Sacred*. Berkeley, California: Conari Press,1998, p. xxvii.

head began to clear, she said, and she felt a little stronger. She kept going and by the time we met her in early July, not only was she walking at our speed, but she looked beautiful, and was speaking perfect English, French, German, Swedish. She glowed with health and energy. The pilgrimage gave her her life back, she said.

"I'm not Catholic, but I use these churches to cry." Her husband was to meet her in a couple of days in Leon, on July 7, nearly three months after she left home. "He won't know me," she said. "I am so transformed."

We also stepped into every church that was on the path, many of them built in the Middle Ages for pilgrims. Many had statues of St. James. We always paused before St. James to give thanks, to touch his feet or cloak. When there was a mass, we went. When there was a pilgrim blessing, we went.

At Rabanal, in Spain on our forty-eighth day, we went to the 7:00 p.m. Vespers and the 9:30 p.m. Compline and Blessing of the Pilgrims sung in Gregorian chant by the three Benedictine monks of Monte Irago. The services were in the tiny Romanesque church of Our Lady built in the twelfth century by the Knights Templar. The voices of the three monks, sometimes one, sometimes two, sometimes all three filled that small holy space crowded with pilgrims. There were leaflets in English, French, German, Spanish, so we could follow along, but we didn't need to. The beauty of the Gregorian chant, the company of our fellow pilgrims, and the sacredness of that simple space were enough. We understood.

Arriving at Monte Do Gozo was a relief. Monte Do Gozo is the first place that the pilgrim can glimpse the spires of the Cathedral of Santiago de Compostela. Traditionally, pilgrims spend the night there, cleanse themselves in the waters of Lavacolla the next day, and then make their way to Santiago. We spent the night there on our first pilgrimage—but we didn't linger the second time. The last days were hard on Chuck; his knee completely gave out; we had to rest frequently. We didn't talk about the possibility that a strong will and courage wouldn't be enough to get him to Santiago. Susan was having a lot of shin pain, her rest stops coincided with ours, and so we walked together the last two days.

The fifty-eighth day started in the rain, in the dark through the eucalyptus forest. It was a bit unnerving, but lovely in its way—the sweet smell of eucalyptus drew us forward and the long pale leaves on the path showed the way. "Quite magical," Susan said, and Chuck complained about walking with a couple of romantics. She stopped for coffee on the outskirts of town and we went on.

It was with full hearts that we held hands and mounted the steps of the cathedral in Santiago and stood just inside the door. The cathedral was packed, a mass had just started, and we saw a friend almost immediately, Roberto, the older Argentinean brother. He embraced us both—"You are here!" he said. Yes, we were there. You tell everybody you are walking to Santiago, but it is as if you don't really expect to arrive. You focus on the walking, on the birds singing, on the steep descent, on the rocky path, on the promise of coffee in the next village, on the hope of seeing somebody you know when you push open the door of the *refugio*, on finding a *boulangerie* to buy bread, on the herd of sheep that follow you for hours as you cross the Pyrenees, on finding the church open when you finally stop for the day. But one day, you arrive.

There are rituals around the pilgrim's arrival in Santiago de Compostela, rituals to remind you of the importance of ritual, of not just arriving and saying, "Well, I made it, here I am." There are things that every pilgrim must do. First, you present yourself at the pilgrim office—yes, there is a pilgrim office—to offer your credentials, your *credenciale*, and to receive the compostela, certification of the completion of the pilgrimage—that you have walked at least the last 100 kilometers.

Then you go to the cathedral and place your hand on the Tree of Jesse under the statue of St. James. The Tree of Jesse is worn and molded by the millions of hands that were placed there before yours—your hand sinks into the imprint of their fingers and palms in the marble. On the other side of the Tree of Jesse is a bust of Mateo, the architect of the great cathedral. You place your forehead against his to gain some of his wisdom, then you walk the length of the nave toward the thirteenth century statue of St. James high on the gold encrusted altar to embrace the saint from behind, the "hug for the apostle," then you descend to a small room under the altar to stand before the silver casket said to hold his bones.

You go to the pilgrim mass at noon that begins with a single woman singing *a capella*, her lovely voice embracing every stone, window, and chapel of the great cathedral. After the homily, the priest announces the pilgrims who have arrived since noon of the previous day—two Americans, he says—*dos Americanos*—arrived this day from Le Puy. If you are lucky, the *Botafumeiro*, a giant, silver incense burner weighing nearly 200 pounds is swung. It requires a team of eight men and an elaborate system of pulleys to swing it from one end of the transept to the other, higher and higher until it nearly touches the ceiling. The swing of the *Botafumeiro* brings you to your feet—they've been swinging it for hundreds of years—and it is swinging for you.

Christine was there. We hadn't seen her in two weeks, but she was there in the cathedral, *una pelegrina de Suecia* had arrived in Santiago from Le Puy that day, the same day we did. She was there with her tall, handsome husband, and she was glowing and at times so emotional that she couldn't speak. She asked how the fortieth day was for us, said it was very hard for her, and then went on to explain the many Biblical references to forty as a time of struggle.

I was moved by her question, by how we search for some larger reference point for our struggle, some reason for things to be so hard, for something not our fault, something not accidental, something that gives meaning . . . and we are still searching on the day of arrival.

We had walked into Santiago with Susan, saw Doug, Lotte and Lona in the plaza, ran into the dour Scot with the red hat whose name we never knew, looked in vain for Jan, the Norwegian, heard from Orling—ray of light—by email that she had gone on to Finisterre, saw Thierry outside a shop and at the bus station, when we were leaving for Madrid to catch our plane home, we ran into Bartholomew, the great communicator, also on his way home. Bartholomew had carried the most elaborately decorated staff of any pilgrim we knew, but he didn't have it with him that day. "Where is your stick?"

"I left it in the cathedral," he said, touching his heart. "A gift for Santiago. I must leave it here."

Of course. The Buddha said, "You cannot travel the path until you have become the path." And you leave—or give—a part of yourself with every step. True of walking the pilgrimage with the cuckoo sounding at the edge of the forest every day, true of walking the labyrinth with the sun streaming through the window, true of walking out of this room today into the next stage, the next *étape*, of our lives.

Reading Poetry

I read poetry. Apparently quite a lot of us do. According to my chief researcher (Google), of the nearly 12 percent of adults who read poetry last year, 70 percent of that audience was under fifty-five. The most popular poet today is the Canadian writer Rupi Kaur, whom I had never heard of until my researcher introduced her to me. Kaur does publish books, but she rose to fame on Instagram (which explains why I, age eighty, was ignorant of her). I do have an Instagram account because my fifty-something offspring said I needed it.

Do I post?

Almost never.

Why?

I love pen and paper, a book in my hand, the printed-on-paper look of a poem. I am stuck in my generation. Give me credit for having the account (and 147 followers, not all of whom are related to me), but don't expect me to post on Instagram or Facebook or, God forbid, Twitter (or whatever it is called now).

Back to poetry. The most powerful book of poetry I've read in the last year is Joy Harjo's anthology of native nations poetry, *When The Light Of The World Was Subdued, Our Songs Came Through*, a book that has made clear the origins of the challenges we face in these fraught times. Harjo presents 159 poetic voices telling their stories in their own time and in their own words. The poem of the earliest poet represented, Eleazar, who died of smallpox in 1678 just before graduating from Harvard, is called "Eleazar's Elegy for Thomas Thacher" and was originally written in Latin. The youngest poet in the collection is Jake Skeets Diné, Black Street Wood, born in 1991.

The line that stopped me, that for many days prevented me from reading further, was "I hate the Grecian poet's song" in William Walker's[28] "Oh, Give Me Back My Bended Bow." That line is not a comment on the inadequacy of ancient Greek poets, but the hubris of the poet's western education denying the validity of his heritage and people on this continent, to replace it with the verse of poets half a world away. Walker was educated in Greek, Latin, French, Wyandot, English, Delaware, Shawnee, Miami, and Potawatomi, published widely and died in 1874. Ever hear of him?

When I was able to continue reading, I read wonderful poems translated from one of the more than 150 indigenous languages or written in English, then was stopped again at Heid Erdrich's[29] "The Theft Outright."

※

Outright. Now there's an interesting word, defined as something given freely, completely, without conditions, no strings attached, being completely or exactly what is stated.[30] You don't need to earn it or deserve it; it is yours. There is an assumption that it will be freely accepted and probably not asked for—just given or taken—because it is right,

---

28. William Walker (HÄH-SHĀH-RÊHS) 1800-1874, Wyandot rights advocate, who served as principal chief of the Wyandot tribe from 1835–36 and the first provisional governor of Nebraska Territory.
29. Heid Erdrich, (1963–) Anishinaabe-Turtle Mountain Band, author of seven collections of poetry and winner of multiple awards and fellowships.
30. Outright: As an adverb: "altogether, completely, immediately. As an adjective, "Open and direct; not concealed; not by degrees or installments; total; complete; undisputed; clear."

or your "right," already owned, yours to have, to keep, to do with what you wish.

So the noun that proceeds "outright," the descriptor or object that precedes the adjective, is all important; the noun bears the weight of meaning. And, for me, the earliest poetic reference to "outright" that I am familiar with is Robert Frost's "The Gift Outright," where the poet references "The deed of gift was many deeds of war." I assume he was thinking of the Revolutionary War, not the Indian wars, wars that resulted in treaties, truces, armistices (soon broken), the forced assimilation, the establishment of reservations, or the Indian Removal Act of 1830 which ended in thousands of deaths and has since been recognized as an act of genocide. Those removals, "the gift outright" and those "many deeds of war" that created the United States, are not present in Frost's amnesiac poem.

He makes no reference to the people living on the land when the Pilgrims landed, and he apparently had forgotten or was ignorant of the first Thanksgiving and the generosity of the Wampanoag who shared an autumn harvest feast with the pilgrims. There is much to admire in Frost's prodigious poetic output, but "The Gift Outright," recited at the inauguration of John F. Kennedy is clear evidence of our hubris as a nation, of our embedded, collective amnesia or ignorance, and, particularly, of the privilege and assumed superiority of white people. "The deed of gift" was indeed *many* deeds of war, and not just against England.

I remember that inauguration and the venerable eighty-six-year-old poet declaiming the poem on a blistery Washington morning. It felt so right for the wise old man to celebrate the young president with his eloquence and to state what he thought obvious: our gift outright. "The land that was not our land," a reference to the white settlers still under the rule of England, and thus a reference to the "owner" of the land, England, more than 3500 miles away; no mention of the Wampanoag who had inhabited that land for 10,000 years and who were still there.

It took 60 years for another inaugural poet, Amanda Gorman, a twenty-two-year-old Black woman, to lay out our challenges, our predicaments, and our possibilities in "The Hill We Climb," a young woman welcoming an aging president to "lift our gazes not to what stands between us/but to what stands before us . . . the hill we climb/if only we dare . . . If only we're brave enough to see it/If only we're brave enough to be it." *At last . . . and amazing.*

Circus of the Damned

We met on the phone: Jimmy, an inmate at Minnesota's level five maximum custody prison, me, an adjunct faculty member at Hamline University in St. Paul. He had earned his GED at El Reno Federal Reformatory in Oklahoma, had no undergraduate credits, yet he talked his way into my graduate level writing class. He couldn't attend the three-hour class meetings, so I audio taped each session, and mailed him the tapes and the student papers to be critiqued for the following week. He called me to discuss the readings every Monday from the Education Director's office at the prison.

I was nervous before that first call, but he made it easy. He sounded like home: distinctly southern, warm and friendly, a gregarious Louisiana Bayou boy talking to an introverted Georgia girl, both of us surprised at finding ourselves in the frigid north. I'd done it the easy way by marrying a Minnesotan. Jimmy's road was considerably harder: he had been bloodied by fellow inmates at USP Leavenworth and transferred to Minnesota for his safety. I didn't know then those were the only free calls he could make. I didn't say much on those calls because he was so very happy to be talking to me, so responsive to everything I suggested, and so grateful to have contact with somebody on the outside, somebody in the world he might never see again . . . unless he escaped.

He was a veteran of multiple escapes from juvenile facilities and was writing a novel based on his escape as an adult from the notorious Louisiana State Penitentiary in Angola. The chapter he submitted to the class was written in the voice of a boastful, muscle-bound narrator with an unfortunate fondness for adverbs and adjectives, a narrator who exaggerated his own prowess in comparison to the faults and stupidity of others. It was awful, but we read it; I taped the class's frank discussion of the manuscript and mailed him the tape along with everybody's written response to his work.

Well, the transformation was notable: Jimmy made the biggest improvement from first draft to revision that I had ever seen. Not only had he heard what had troubled me and his classmates, but he also understood what we saw as powerful and engaging; he had beautifully re-imagined and rewritten the chapter. He was a good student in other ways: enthusiastic, incisive, and genuinely helpful in comments on fellow students' writing, an appreciative reader of the assignments, and a hard worker. He earned that A.

※

That was more than 30 years ago.

He now calls from Rayburn Correctional Facility, a medium security prison in Angie, Louisiana, where he earns two cents an hour as night orderly for the his Unit Key, the central area between four dorms. He keeps the Key clean and when a man is sent to the hole, he transports their locker and mattress. He also brews coffee for the Key officers—a perk because he's allowed to drink it. So it's good duty, better than being a pusher, the guy who pushes a wheelchair for another inmate. Pushers don't mind helping the paraplegic man or the one with both legs amputated, but they avoid Billy[31] who treats his pushers

---

31. The names of all the men referenced, except for Jimmy's, have been changed.

like servants: "empty my pee jar," he'll demand. Many of the men in Jimmy's unit are ambulatory, if you include the ones with walkers, the three dragging CO_2 tanks behind them, or the ones with cancer. Even the blind guy gets around on his own, but too many have HIV, one so emaciated Jimmy calls him "Walking Bones," and almost all of the seventy-four old men in his dorm are in the pill line twice a day. He calls it the Circus of the Damned.

Jimmy's been a member of this circus, this sideshow, this spectacle of the lost since he was thirteen years old and sent to reform school for skipping school and joy riding. "Now you'll learn how to behave," the judge said. It was a prophetic statement; he did learn how to behave. At thirteen, Jimmy was a slight kid with a taste for exploration, adventure, and avoidance; he didn't do well in school, so he skipped, but he was never mean, never a bully, never a fighter. He didn't need a roughneck persona until he arrived at LTI (Louisiana Training Institute) Monroe. There he learned how to fight, how never to show fear, and how to escape. These were accomplishments that, through a series of demerits for fighting, for escaping from reformatories and stealing cars to facilitate those escapes, extended his time behind bars to cover his entire adolescence and also sent him to a variety of federal institutions. "Training schools for gladiators," he says. By the time he was released at age twenty-two, he was well prepared for the life reformatories had educated him for: drugs, drink, and tough guy swagger.

On July 12, 1982, he entered a deli with a non-firing Civil War replica pistol jammed in his belt. According to store employees, he demanded money, one of them emptied the cash register of $136, he grabbed it, and left. He was arrested fourteen days later. There were many irregularities at his trial: his lawyer, under disbarment proceedings at the time, didn't object to a psychiatrist who admitted that his testimony "had nothing to do with the law," but said Jimmy was "anti-social" and "must go to jail." The judge took note and when Jimmy was found guilty, sentenced him to **eighty years at hard labor without benefit of parole, probation, or suspension of sentence.** It was his first adult conviction. A week later he was on his way to Angola prison.

So it's a complicated story, with many twists and turns, some precipitated by Jimmy's reputation for hot feet—his escape record—and others by the tragedy that is our criminal justice system.

※

His escape from Angola in 1986 earned him a tour of federal prisons in addition to the detour to Minnesota, but he finished his federal sentences in 2016 and was transported back to Louisiana to finish out the eighty-year sentence. He immediately filed for an evidentiary hearing to consider the multiple errors at his original trial, including representation by a lawyer disbarred for incompetence, a misreading of his history of transfers as a juvenile that made it look as if he had been charged for a new crime every time he was transferred, and an excessive sentence for a robbery in which nobody was hurt and $136 taken. The judge granted him the evidentiary hearing which the Assistant DA appealed, claiming prejudice because the disbarred lawyer was dead and could not testify. Jimmy was sure the appeal would be denied and made plans to move into an apartment his sister offered him in Shreveport. After seventeen months of waiting, the appeal was upheld on February 11, 2019; the evidentiary hearing was denied. It's over, his court appointed attorney said.

But nothing is ever over for James Colvin. It is his life that is at stake, and he fights for it every day. In May of 2019, he filed a Motion to Amend the Sentence, submitted a habeas corpus petition in federal court to challenge the constitutionality of his eighty-year sentence, and prepared a civil suit submitted to the 22nd Judicial District Court in Washington Parish, arguing that his federal time served should be concurrent with his state time served. He also filed a new application for post-conviction relief under LA. C. Cr. P. Art 930.8(A)(2), regarding a new constitutional rule handed down by the Supreme Court in *McCoy v. Louisiana*. He has learned the law, researched what applies in his case, and filed petition after petition without legal help.

On July 11, 2019, his application for post-conviction relief was denied as untimely, meaning it was submitted late, which is not true. It was delivered to the court on May 13, 2019, making the deadline by one day, but the clerk stamped it received two days later and so the application was rejected without being considered.

Every time he describes his latest filing, he assures me that this is the ticket, this is the one that will set him free or, at least, shorten his sentence. He's got it now; figured it out now, and has been disappointed time after time.

He's working to live as a free man, but he is also working to create a meaningful life wherever he is. His interest in Catholicism has blossomed in recent years. On March 12, 2019, he wrote "I want to start a religious order of contemplative monks for anyone in here, especially for those guys who are long dead to the world and have nothing but God." When the Archbishop of New Orleans celebrated mass in the prison, Jimmy thanked him, and later wrote him, described his long incarceration and said, "with your help and support, I could grow a serious religious order for men who have nothing else in life but to serve God's will. It must be a serious life vocation . . ."

The Archbishop replied: "In any situation, the founding of a religious order is difficult and proceeds very slowly. There must be at least three, preferably four, persons who desire to take the initial steps to form a community, and someone who can guide their formation and evaluate their progress." The Archbishop asked a nun to consult with the spiritual director of the Discalced Carmelites about the possibility.

Jimmy was elated. He has found seven other inmates who are interested and is waiting to hear from the Sister about next steps. He intends to continue the work of forming a religious order even if he is released, and if not, he will have found meaning and purpose in spite of being incarcerated.

Jimmy is not the only person in the old men's unit struggling with self-preservation.

Jeremiah, eighty-two years old, can't stand up straight, showers bent over holding onto a railing. Jeremiah has fifteen years for drug possession. He was pulled over, his car searched, prescription pills found, and one hit of crack on a female passenger. He was up for parole recently, but denied because he had an Ensure drink in his locker; he's supposed to drink it at the pill-line window.

David has some affliction that makes him work his jaw and move his head as if he is chewing something huge. Few can understand him. He also razor-cuts patches in his hair, making multiple bald spots on his scalp. Jimmy says he looks like a stressed cockatoo who's pulled out his feathers.

❋

Chuck and I have visited Jimmy in Louisiana three times. The first time, after we left, a guard asked him why someone would come all the way from Minnesota to see him. He smiled and said, "They are my friends, and I am a pretty good old guy. Besides, if you got to know me, you might visit me too."

Yes, he's a pretty good old guy, and not the only old guy who belongs at home. The recidivism rate for felons over sixty is less than five percent and close to zero for those who, like Jimmy and Jeremiah, were convicted of non-violent crimes. Jimmy's sister has an apartment waiting for him. Why can't he go home?

Well, he won't give up. Jimmy fights for his life every day. During the day he researches the law. At night, he keeps the Unit Key clean, makes the coffee, and, on a quiet evening, has a cup himself. We're both waiting, waiting for the day when every call doesn't start with a ninety second recording: "This is a call from a Louisiana Correctional Facility . . ."

NOTE: This essay appeared in the October/November 2019 issue of *The Progressive* magazine. It's 2025 now, and Jimmy is still at Rayburn Correctional Center. He has multiple health issues, a pacemaker, and syncope (a tendency for a sudden loss of consciousness—fainting—which can be caused by problems at several places in the heart's electrical system). In mid-August of last year he was sitting outside[32] with a couple of other inmates when he fainted. The other guys put him in a wheelchair that was nearby, wheeled him to a guard, who took him to the clinic, where they assumed he was intoxicated and Narcaned him—it is not uncommon for drugs to be smuggled into a prison. When he revived, they sent him to Disciplinary where he was sentenced to eighteen days in the hole for being intoxicated. He *repeatedly* asked for a urine test to prove that he was not intoxicated, pointed out that fainting was common for somebody with his medical conditions (which is clear in his medical records which the prison has). They refused his repeated requests for a urine test, and put him in the hole, a five foot by seven foot cell with another inmate, with no ability to spend time in the yard.

Kathleen with Jimmy, circa 2020

---

32. The temperature that day was in the 90s with high humidity. There is no air conditioning at Rayburn in any of the areas the inmates are able to be in.

When Death Comes

✤

A word about "that cottage of darckness,[33]*" death. When a friend died unexpectedly in his sleep, a mutual friend told me she hoped to die that way, in her sleep, without pain or fear.*

*I don't. I want to know I am entering that "cottage of darkness," the final experience of my life. I want to be able to say goodbye to my beloved family and friends, to tell them I love them, but it is also **my** final experience on this earth. I want to know it is happening, even to savor it, this new road, new path, my entry into a new part of the universe of... what? Particles? Energy? Writer Aaron Freeman*[34] *reminds us, "No energy gets created in the universe, and none is destroyed." That means me. That means you. We are all included.*

---

33. Op. Cit., Oliver, "When Death Comes."
34. Op.Cit., Freeman.

The Gift

Lizzie, a middle-aged, reclusive, gray feline, was a gift, a gift who arrived with considerable assets. Her accoutrements included two litter boxes: one with a hut-shaped shield that fit over the tray that held the perfumed grit, the other a more modest low-rise affair; a cardboard carrying case for transporting her; 25 pounds of kitty litter; 20 pounds of Friskie's Original Recipe dried cat food; a ceramic water dish; two square plastic food bowls; a hair brush; and a tiny basket woven with blue and gold metallic thread and filled with ten round sparkling puffs. We were told the puffs were the only toy she liked, and the exotic basket came from Kenya—a bonus gift.

Chuck and I hadn't had a pet in twenty years and didn't know what cats in the twenty-first century required, so we accepted her personal effects gratefully, relieved that she had no apparel, no dear little booties, no sweaters, no scarves. We aren't the sort of people who dress animals, but then neither was Dorothy, Lizzie's previous owner. Dorothy was spare, meticulous, well-organized, didn't believe in having what you didn't need. She didn't have a dishwasher—the kitchen sink worked just fine—or a clothes dryer—the sun dried the clothes just fine—or a television. She read books, played the piano, listened to music, made art, talked to her friends, wrote essays, taught literature, went to museums, and filled a hundred journals longhand.

In late June, Dorothy called a meeting of twenty-one friends. She was just home from a rough week at the hospital, very rough, and was beginning home hospice care. The group gathered in her small living room were college professors, lawyers, publishers, teachers, writers, ministers, and artists, and we were nervous. The approach of death does that to the healthy. We all expected to see summer fade into fall, to watch the leaves change color, to set our clocks back. We expected to vote for the next president of the United States and to eat turkey at Thanksgiving. Dorothy did not expect to do any of those things. We were humble, in new territory, afraid, not only for Dorothy, but for ourselves. Afraid we wouldn't know how to help her.

She came out on the arm of her son Andy, both of them bright-eyed and smiling. Dorothy was not given to drama, but she made an entrance that day, laughing when she pointed out that she had put on her "good" robe for the occasion, a gorgeous, long red brocade. She looked like herself, tall, thin, alert, her short hair curving around her small head like the curls etched on a Greek statue. She never used makeup, never saw the need for it and carried herself with confidence. She thanked us for coming and got right to the point. "I have a gift for you," she said. "I want you to take care of me." Both sons lived out of town. They would be with her as often as they could, but she needed help twenty-four seven. That was the gift. She gave us her bright smile, Andy helped her back to her room, and we got busy. Shari and Nikki had read *Share the Care: How to Organize a Group to Care for Someone Who Is Seriously Ill*, they described a possible organizational structure, we agreed to four-hour shifts, Denny set up a communications system, Linda and I made schedules, we all learned how to use the nebulizer and what to say if we called 911.

When our shifts started, Dorothy was clear and specific. She said what needed cleaning, washing, dusting, what she wanted to eat, when she wanted to sleep, when she wanted a bath or a foot rub. Her clarity was a blessing because none of us were ever left wondering how to help a dying woman we loved. The single most important thing we all learned was how to make sure Lizzie never stepped outside. There was a brick on the back porch that you slid against the screen door every time you went outside so Lizzie couldn't unintentionally push the door open and find herself in alien territory. She was a house cat and had no interest in the world beyond, but there was a remote chance that she might accidentally find herself on the wrong side of a door if one of us failed to close it properly. We were all amused by Dorothy's very specific rules for her cat. Dorothy was a fearless traveler; she had visited every continent, had biked in Havana, had shimmied down the Cu Chi tunnels outside Hanoi, and much more, but Lizzie was not to leave the house.

Sheila, the hospice nurse, came twice a week. During a visit in early August, Dorothy spent the first ten minutes quizzing Sheila about her family, her husband's daffodil farm, her cold, until finally Sheila steered the conversation to Dorothy. "What are you worried about?" Sheila asked.

"Lizzie," Dorothy said. Neither son could take her and who would want an old cat. Which is when I raised my hand and said that I would want an old cat, if Dorothy could trust me with her. "Yes," Dorothy said. "Your house is perfect."

※

The twenty-block trip from Dorothy's house to my house was not perfect for Lizzie. It was grueling. She moaned and trembled and when we finally got home and let her out of the box, she hid. We let her go, knew she needed to sniff about on her own, but when we looked for her later, it took four adults with flashlights thirty minutes to locate her under the pipes between the basement wall and the washing machine. We pulled her out, showed her the litter box (low-rise version), her familiar water and food dishes, and threw out a puff ball (her favorite toy) to play with. She fled.

The second half-hour search—same four adults with flashlights—found her lined up with the shoes and shoe brushes on a narrow shelf under the basement stairs.

She was missing again when we got up the next morning. Her food was untouched, the litter box undisturbed. Another half-hour search. I talked to her this time, assured her of our good intentions, brushed her with her own hairbrush. Her fur came off in handfuls; she hadn't been brushed in weeks. I begged her to eat, but she wasn't interested. She didn't eat for five days. She was grieving.

Well, so were we. Dorothy died exactly one week after she'd said goodbye to Lizzie. I told Lizzie of course, but it wasn't news to her. She knew Dorothy was gone. She'd lost her the moment we stuffed her in the awful carry box and put her in our car. The handfuls of cat hair that came out when I brushed her showed that nobody had been petting or brushing her those last weeks. We'd protected her from what she didn't want—going outside—but Dorothy had grown too weak to have Lizzie in her lap and those days that we were doing our shifts, coming and going, Lizzie didn't want to be with anybody else.

The second week, Lizzie picked at her food but spent her days and nights in the basement, sitting in a narrow place between the sofa and the wall. If you pulled her out, she went back. She didn't cry or meow or purr. She didn't play with the fluffy toy things that we distributed strategically about the house.

We assumed that she was, by nature, an aloof animal—cats often are—and she'd seemed pretty solitary at Dorothy's. We learned her hiding places, checked on her a couple of times a day, and left her alone. She came upstairs for the first time the day there was a meeting in my dining room of six of the caregivers to plan Dorothy's funeral. She recognized the voices, knew we were talking about Dorothy, and watched us from the living room. After some time, she jumped up on Linda's lap. She'd always liked Linda.

After that, she sat on my lap when I was reading or knitting, just sat there, silent, lost in her memories. Dorothy read a lot; it made sense that Lizzie liked to sit in the lap of a woman with a book. Everybody asked about Lizzie at the funeral in late September, and I told them she was fine, really fine. I bragged about how well Lizzie had adjusted in only a month. I hadn't adjusted to Dorothy's death quite so quickly, but Lizzie, well, Lizzie was just a cat, our cat now. She was fine, herself, back to normal, I said. She had even given up hiding. She wasn't particularly affectionate, but her fur no longer came off in handfuls, and she was consuming half a dish of Friskie's Original a day.

✼

I dreamed about Dorothy one night, three months after she died, nothing specific, just that she was there in her kitchen, in an ethereal light that illuminated her just enough for me to know it was she, and that she was at home, not surprised to see me, not saying much, just there, and then gone. She had never inhabited my dreams when she was alive, so I appreciated her checking in on me now—or maybe it was Lizzie she was checking up on. She didn't mention Lizzie in the dream, but her unexpected appearance made me reconsider Lizzie's adjustment.

"You're getting a wonderful cat," Dorothy had said. Those last words came back to me often, especially after Lizzie seemed "normal" because she hadn't seemed all that wonderful at the beginning. Rather distant is how I would describe her. But since Dorothy's appearance in my dream, it occurred to me a month later that Lizzie *was* quite wonderful. She waited at the door when I came home, she rolled over on her back, presented herself to be petted, caressed, loved. She purred, loudly and insistently. She followed us around waiting for somebody to sit down so she could climb up. She meowed when we opened the refrigerator door.

One night, she engaged in one of those ridiculous gymnastics that cats do, chasing her tail. She went on for some time then suddenly realized it was her own tail she was pursuing. She stopped, showed no embarrassment, pretended she had known all along that it was her tail, licked her right paw, and washed her face.

She also developed a heightened curiosity about every open

drawer or door. She became demanding. She meowed when we opened the refrigerator door, was indignant if we sat down to supper without offering her a bite. Dorothy had been explicit about treats for Lizzie, one spoon, one spoon only, of Friskie's Salmon Supper at 6:00 p.m., but Lizzie claimed she needed more.

Lizzie became herself, curious, independent, an affectionate purring machine, a real cat, a cat who might just wander outside if the door were left ajar, a cat who needed months to mourn the loss of the woman who raised her, who loved her, who knew her best, who smelled the way a person should smell, whose voice resonated with Lizzie. The stages of grief for an animal haven't been closely documented, but there they were for me to see and learn from. All Lizzie knew was that she had lost the one person she loved the most. I had been surprised when Dorothy said her biggest worry was Lizzie, but Dorothy knew the rest of us would get along without her, knew we had read books about grief, knew we had the funeral to help us, even knew her two boys who would miss her the most, would find solace in their partners, in their children, in all that she had left them of her. But all Lizzie would know was that she was abandoned, lost, the door open at last, and her on the wrong side of it.

Lizzie did what we all do when we are bereft, when we can't understand what has happened, when we don't want to know: we moan, we hide, we lose ourselves until time and routine and new loves slowly settle in, and we become whole again. Lizzie didn't forget Dorothy. She sat at the window waiting for her to come home. But when it was only I who stepped through the door, she rolled over so I could rub her stomach. It was clear that she saw Dorothy in that dream too and knew that she was all right. Lizzie became a wonderful cat.

We adjusted too. Chuck and I didn't know we needed a cat, but Lizzie brought a new tenderness to our lives. We needed the warmth of her purring body in our laps, the feel of her arched head. We even needed her walking across our bodies at night as she searched for the warmest niche, the most comfortable corner of our bed. A new routine and a new love filled our lives too. Another gift from Dorothy.

Close Encounters

"I would have gone," Mother said. "I would have followed those creatures right up that ramp onto the ship." We had just seen *Close Encounters of the Third Kind* and were still in the spell of the movie.

I was surprised but shouldn't have been. By the time we saw *Close Encounters* together, I was the well-traveled one—Africa, South America, sliver of Asia, much of Europe, but I knew I would never follow aliens half my size—or any size—onto their space ship.

My mother would. She was curious, adventurous, and not afraid of much. She was also sick for thirty years, sick with mycobacterioses and bronchiectasis, the diseases that finally took her at eighty, but she lived longer than any doctor predicted. "I'm not done yet," she said more than once, her voice as clear and full-throated as ever, even with, or in spite of, the tubes in her nose and the oxygen tank at her side. She was nearly kicked out of hospice because she was living too long. Her hospice provider required a six-month window, and she pushed it to nine before going quietly into that good night.

My brother was there. My father was there. I was in a plane at 30,000 feet trying to be there. I'm not sad or angry that she didn't wait. Just surprised. Her will was that strong. Maybe she didn't hear them say I was coming.

❊

The last time I saw her, six weeks before she died, she had me help her into her dressing room and onto the stool in front of the counter-to-ceiling, wall-to-wall mirror. Getting to the stool and then sitting on it, even supporting herself with both arms on the counter, required enormous effort. She had no muscular strength, but she was determined. She peered into what I called the starlet mirror, one of those stand-alone mirrors with round light bulbs lining both sides of the mirror. "Shave my neck," she said.

I protested: she hadn't left the house in months, her bed in weeks except for trips to the bathroom, and her wardrobe consisted of rotating sets of pajamas. Nobody saw her but family, and we just saw her from the front, lying in bed, propped up on pillows, never the nape of her neck. I said her neck looked fine, didn't need shaving, thought she'd be more comfortable in bed.

"Do it," she croaked. She propped her elbows on the counter and lowered her head to her hands so her pale, thin neck was exposed. Her beautiful hair was flattened against her skull from all the time in bed; the wisps on her neck were barely visible, but I did as directed. Of course I did. There weren't many times in my life when I didn't do what she told me to do. Maybe no times.

When I finished, she ran a shaky finger along the back of her neck. "Thank you," she said. "That's better."

Then she laughed. "How do I look?"

By then, she had lived years beyond her doctor's expectations, not complaining, never telling me how she really felt. When I called and asked how she was, she always laughed and said, "Terrific." She laughed because it was such a ridiculous thing to say. She hadn't been terrific in years, but the closest she would come to admitting she felt rotten all the time was that ironic little laugh when she said, "Terrific."

So when she asked how she looked, pale, short of breath, holding up her head with trembling hands to stare at me in the mirror, when she said, "How do I look?" I said, "Terrific."

※

She was of a generation in which how a woman looked was all important, and she had the good fortune to be beautiful. She had two older sisters, both attractive women, but she was the beauty in the family, the Irish beauty with her dark, curly hair, bright blue eyes, and radiant smile. When I was young, my friends often said, *Your mother is so pretty* or *Your mother looks just like Jackie Kennedy*. I realize that when I talk about her, I usually mention how good-looking she was. She was, but I think that description limits her, then I ask myself, what were all those mirrors and starlet lights about?

Well, appearance mattered to her. She didn't feel dressed without makeup on. She never vacuumed without her nose powdered, never answered the door without fresh lipstick, never left the house without the full face on. "You feel better," she said. "You're not really dressed without it," she said. Her statements about the fundamental importance of makeup increased as it became clear that I lacked a basic interest in powder, foundation, lipstick.

Her criticisms of me almost always focused on my appearance. Many sentences began, "You would be so pretty if you . . ." When I was a teenager, she hated my teased hair—*I can't put my hand anywhere and touch your head*. She told me to spend less time soaking in the tub and more time on my face. "I guess you like the natural look," she'd say, the note of disapproval clear in her tone. She took me to a dermatologist to undergo weekly X-ray therapy for what I now know was a pretty average case of adolescent acne. To her credit, she apologized years later when it was discovered that that particular treatment is linked to cancer of the esophagus.

She also had a great regard for accuracy. One night, as I was about to leave the house, Dad said I looked gorgeous. She quickly corrected him, "Don't be ridiculous, Walt. She doesn't look *gorgeous*. She looks nice, very, very nice." I was glad to look very, very nice, without qualifications, with no mention of my lack of mascara, of my ignorance of blush, of my fine hair that never framed my face right, teased or not.

※

Her thick, wavy hair was washed and set once a week by Robert, a man so politically conservative that she returned from his salon each Saturday in a fury, enraged that anybody could be so narrow, so selfish, so blind, so *stupid*. Twenty-five years into the relationship, she also began complaining about the way he cut her hair, said he was behind the times, hadn't evolved with the styles, but she continued to make the weekly trek to his salon until she was too weak to get in the car. She relished the hour with Robert, because he was as formidable a debater as she was, deliciously wrong about virtually everything, and he kept her looking good.

One afternoon, on my last visit, I glimpsed her unawares, slumped in a chair, looking one hundred three, impossibly old, unable to fill her lungs, worn, jowly, more dead than alive, but when she sensed my presence, her head shot up, and she gave me her dazzling smile. It was then that I realized the smile was the source of her enormous appeal. She had the regular features and slim, curvy body we require in beautiful women, but it was the smile that lit her up, that said, yes, I am beautiful. The smile and the spirit behind it had been her secret, and I had never really seen it—or her—until I witnessed the transformation from crone, hag, dying woman to beauty in the flash of a moment. She was too proud to be caught as less than herself.

※

Only once did she admit to me how very sick she was. "I never thought I'd end up like this," she said, meaning dragging an oxygen tank behind her, in pain, unable to breathe, unable to walk to her own mailbox. The loss of the weekly trips to Robert was especially hard on her . . . the hospice nurse didn't do her hair right, and there was nobody to argue politics with. I don't know what she said to Dad; he was the one she snapped at when it got to be too much, but she never complained to me.

Dad worked for one company his whole life, Lockheed Aircraft Corporation, where he started as a bicycle messenger in the mail room and retired as Director of Marketing, a VIP. He looked good, wore a suit and tie to work every day, a suit and tie to church every Sunday, but it was his slovenly (her word) appearance around the house that bothered her. He wasn't embarrassed to wear an old pair of slacks to the grocery store, to mow the lawn in a shirt dappled with paint stains, or a frayed cap while pumping gas. "Oh, Walt," she'd say as he headed to Home Depot, "you're not wearing that, are you?"

*

When I was alone with him on those visits, he spent most of our time together describing how hard life was with her; and when I was alone with her, she gave me detailed accounts of the trials of living with him. Small, petty details from both of them, burden of the caregiver and the cared for. He also found space to say, with admiration in his voice, how tough she was.

And she found space to say how grateful she was to him. He wanted to move to a condo, but she was too private a person to move to a senior building, to assisted living. She needed him in order to stay in their house and was thankful for him—when she wasn't complaining about his imperfections—which, as I think about it, were mostly about his appearance. She knew, appreciated, and often told me what a good man he was.

*

George Bush—W—was directly responsible for her outliving the six-month hospice boundary. She couldn't stomach Bush, and Al Gore didn't even live up to her standards; she willed herself to make it to election day, to cast her vote for Ralph Nader, and died a month later. For most of her life, she maintained a regular correspondence with her representatives in Washington, taking them to task and offering advice when she felt they needed it. She was never represented by someone she had voted for, and given who represented Georgia's sixth congressional district—Newt Gingrich when she died—she was proud never to have voted for a local winner.

※

She told stories. Her parents—Scottish mother, Irish father—moved the family from Winnipeg to Los Angeles in 1927 when she was seven years old. Several of her father's brothers—he was one of seventeen—were already there. She seemed to remember every detail of their daily life as well as the momentous events: the early death of Uncle Jack's young wife Cis, her father being out of work during the entire Depression. She told the stories vividly, laughing often, and wrote them down in her last years. Along with her disdain for George W., writing those stories kept her going. She was precise, slow, careful. She worried over every phrase. I encouraged her to "just write" because I was eager to have as many stories as possible. But she couldn't do that, couldn't let one story go and start on the next until she was sure the first was perfect. She sent some of them to her sister, Maude, and was infuriated when Maude corrected a detail, questioned the unfolding of an event, or had a different take on what had happened. "I sent them to her to *read*," she fumed, "not to edit."

※

I lingered at the end of that visit, not knowing it was the last time I would see her alive, but knowing it could be, and tried to find something suitably significant and loving to say. Neither of us were much good at articulating our emotions. In our world, you didn't utter, "Love you!" as you parted. I don't know that she ever told me she loved me; I don't know that I ever told her that I loved her—but I did, and she did. Dad called her a dour Scotswoman, and that was true. She was careful

My Mother, Bettie McClintock Johnson

not to overstate, never to offer a gratuitous compliment, but she was also skilled at offering praise where praise was due. She made a point of letting me know she had had a good life, that she was proud of our family, that we'd done well, my brother and I, that she had no regrets. "We had a good family, didn't we? The four of us?"

It was easy to say yes, we did. This decidedly undomestic woman beheld our family, the four of us—father, mother, daughter, son—as the best part of her life.

As I turned to go that day, she rose up from her pillow, looked me over one last time, and said, "I'm glad you never got fat." Her last words to me.

Praise enough. I was glad too.

*

Writing about my mother, perhaps writing about anybody you loved and knew for fifty-seven years is revealing. I find myself gravitating to the odd detail, to stories I've been telling for years, perhaps getting close to her, but missing the mark more often than hitting it. She was a complicated person as we all are. Born too early. Twenty years later and she would have gone to college and been a writer or artist, a teacher or historian. She read widely, was smart, curious, impassioned, said she would be a dancer in her next life, and was eager to walk up a ramp into a spaceship with aliens.

Which is what she did that December day in the first year of the new century. I don't believe in a physical heaven, and I don't think she did either, but when I think of her ready to follow beings from another world, creatures who would dance with her, it's not hard to believe that's where she is right now, dancing her heart out, all these years after we buried her cremains in the lovely garden next to Central Presbyterian Church in Atlanta, Georgia.

A Simple Man

My father carried only one picture of our family: my mother sitting on a stone bench in a park, right leg crossed over left, knee-length skirt, strappy sandals, holding my brother swaddled in a loose blanket on her lap. I am sitting next to her, my right leg crossed over my left in perfect imitation of hers.

The old man transfered this picture from one old wallet to its replacement for 58 years.

The print got battered, but the love never wore out

After Dad died, my brother enlarged the creased black and white photo, framed it, and sent it to me with a note: *"The old man transferred this picture from one old wallet to its replacement for 58 years. The print got battered, but the love never wore out."*

Which captures my father perfectly. My brother too, I might add. *The love never wore out.*

※

My dad was a gentle man, a kind man, shy, unassuming, but successful in the way that a bright, hard-working high school graduate raised during the Depression could be. He retired as Director of Marketing in a large, multinational corporation; you could spend days in his company without knowing anything, but what a nice guy he was, an unimpressive, quiet man who loved Patsy Cline, corny jokes and, forgive me, puns.

He wasn't one to talk about the details of his life. Anything we know of his early life came from Mother, who heard the stories from his older sister. He never mentioned that he was engaged before he met Mother or that his fiancée died in his arms. He was a Seaman 5th class on the USS Missouri where the armistice ending World War II was signed, said his quarters were unpleasant . . . end of story. Mother was the storyteller; he the appreciative listener. Like all good narrators, she told stories more than once, but he listened as if for the first time, appreciating her gift. He thought I was gorgeous, my husband a great guy, our children brilliant, our grandchildren amazing. Those were the kinds of things he told us. That and the jokes. He always had a new joke when he called, so the evening I answered the phone, and he said, "I'm getting married," I waited for the next part of the story, the joke, the punch line.

No joke. He had met Alice at a celebration of residents with September birthdays at the senior complex where he lived after Mother died . . . and they were getting married. Soon! He was eighty-four; she eighty-two. As I said in my wedding toast to them, "Most of us don't get to see our father as a teenager, head over heels in love, romantic, finding coincidences in everything . . . their birthdays on the same day, the same picture hanging on the wall in their living rooms. Even Alice, something of a teenager herself in this story, said it was going too far when he suggested that the fact that they owned similar letter openers meant they should spend the rest of their lives together. So, I thought, I'm seeing a new side of my father. Aren't I lucky?"

※

I *was* lucky. I knew it because Mother reminded me so often. Her family had emigrated to California just in time for the Depression—her quick-to-anger, alcoholic father didn't work for years, her mother cleaned other people's houses. In fact, she mentioned our good luck so frequently that it became a source of anxiety for her. She worried that our childhood was too easy, uneventful, formless, that my brother and I were deficient somehow, without character. What would become of a person who had nothing to form them? Growing up in the suburbs in a nice house with calm, fully employed parents—a father who was never angry or mean or critical or drunk, and me with never a concern about how the family was going to pay the bills or keep a roof over our heads. Lucky, that's what I was.

I felt lucky until I read that Hemingway said the two requisites for a writer were an unhappy childhood and the experience of war. I didn't expect to serve in combat and had a crisis-free childhood—handicapped forever as a writer and, perhaps, as a human being. Mother did remind me—often—that I wasn't perfect, so it was *her* opinion that mattered, *her* approval I craved, *her* praise that made a difference. More than once, Dad said I was gorgeous, smart, wonderful, but I had a mirror; I knew what I looked like; I knew my shortcomings; I knew whose judgment mattered.

I've thought about this often, about how much weight we give to criticism and how lightly we can hold love or praise freely given. Since

Dad always thought I was wonderful—clearly untrue—I didn't take him seriously; it was what Mother thought and said that counted. She too offered her share of praise, but less dependably, and often with a qualification—*you would be so pretty if you* . . .

*

It took me years to fully appreciate my father. When I mentioned this to my brother, he said, "Well, Mother was more interesting." That's true; she was more interesting, more outspoken, more demanding, better looking, the star of the family, the one in charge.

Dad was sweet and dependable. Never angry. I only remember him raising his voice once. Mother was playing the piano in the living room, and our dog Alexander was sitting next to the piano howling as he always did when somebody played. It was predictable: when you struck the first key on the piano, Alexander appeared out of nowhere, threw his head back, and howled.

Suddenly Dad was on the stairs, shouting, "I'm trying to take a nap!"

We were so surprised to see him there in his blue terrycloth bathrobe hollering—such an unlikely sight—that we all laughed. Mother did stop playing; the dog stopped howling; but we laughed and laughed. We didn't mean to be cruel, but the shock of seeing him mad enough to raise his voice and the incongruity of him in his bathrobe yelling in the middle of a sunny afternoon was too much.

I feel compelled to note that nobody would have been laughing if had been Mother angry and shouting. We were more accustomed to her temper, more wary, more careful. But Dad? He took me by surprise. I've always felt guilty about laughing that time—his complaint was legitimate—it was the surprise of his raised voice that set me off—and, of course, Mother laughed too, made a joke of it, didn't say "sorry."

Which is not to say that he was never irritated. He was. In his later years, I was to hear complaints about this and that—mostly about how difficult Mother was—between the time he picked me up at the MARTA station until we got to their house. And when I was alone with her, I heard her litany of complaints about him. Those last years were hard, Mother ill and so dependent on him; they both had plenty to complain about, but Mother never ended her stream without saying, "Well, I don't know what I would do without him." And he always ended with a comment about her courage, her toughness, the dour Scot in her.

But Dad having a meltdown, an emotional outburst? Shouting? Yelling? Only that one time.

※

The summer I worked at Lockheed, we rode in to work together. He was so pleased to have me, his daughter, in the car with him twice a day; he loved talking to me, hearing about my day. I confess to being unresponsive at times, not forthcoming, aware that he was so happy to be with me and not wanting to encourage it. It's hard to explain or even understand now. I was nineteen years old, should have been more mature, but I held back, didn't offer him all the conversation he was hungry for; I was polite, but there was something in me that didn't want to give too much, a hesitation I was barely conscious of, but I know it was there. Even so, that was the summer I came to realize that he had more—a lot more—to him than the man I saw puttering around the house, cutting the grass, putting in a patio.

At Lockheed, he parked in the reserved parking lot, the guards all knew his name and his office was large, very large, and well furnished—elegant even—unlike the cubicle in the cluster of desks and file cabinets that I spent time in. I was a file clerk that summer, a mind-numbing job, sorting, alphabetizing, and filing endless stacks of documents in a huge room with row after row after row of files.

Dad clearly had a more interesting job. I commented to Mother that he seemed important at work, that everybody knew him, called him Mr. Johnson, and more than one person was impressed to know I was his daughter.

"Not like the old man who slouches around here in work pants with paint on them," she said.

"No," I said, a bit mystified at how this quiet, unassuming guy ended up in what apparently was quite a significant position. I didn't get it.

Until he rose to give the toast at my wedding. I would have said that Mother was the obvious choice; she was the eloquent one, but in those days, it had to be the father who toasted the new couple.

He stood. I held my breath. People quieted. He smiled, looked around and began to speak. I can't tell you his words, but they were from the heart, full of both love and eloquence, exactly right. Perfect, in fact. The words of a loving, bright man who could inspire others to be their best selves, to do their best work, to follow his lead because not only was he eloquent, he was a simple man of unquestioned integrity, and you knew that what he said was right.

I began to see him then as the man he was—quiet, yes. Plain spoken, yes. And eloquent. Smart. Loving. I only heard him speak publicly a few times after that, at my brother's wedding, my children's weddings, Mother's funeral, before his own marriage to Alice, but when I held my breath then, it wasn't because I was worried; it was because I knew I was about to hear something wonderful.

In his eulogy for Dad, my brother said, "He was a simple person, with a straightforward soul. He didn't give advice, he lived it. He came from plain stock. His carpenter father spent most of the Depression years out of work, the family a few steps ahead of poverty. Dad worked with one company for thirty-four years, starting out of high school as a bike messenger at the Lockheed plant in Burbank and retiring an executive with hundreds reporting to him, and the responsibility to sell those huge planes to the Belgians, the Saudis, the U.S. government.

"He loved his family. He didn't need to tell us. We knew. We knew that if we were smart in school or stupid in love, Dad loved us."

I knew that too—always, that Dad loved us, but I didn't think much about it, didn't value that love, didn't know the richness that was mine until he was gone. I knew he was smart, an eloquent speaker even, but he was so easy, so appreciative, so uncritical, so unassuming. So underappreciated. Wonderful things were said about Mother at her funeral—by Dad, by me, by the minister. "I wonder what you'll say about me," Dad said that day. I didn't really think about it or wonder about it then—what would there be to say? Mother was the interesting one.

Well, he was more than a cliché. That's what I learned when I googled "quiet man poem," thinking I could insert some words here that described Dad perfectly, that showed I finally appreciated him, but what you would expect is out there, all Father's Day card-worthy:

> *He never looks for praises*
> *He's never one to boast*
> *He just goes on quietly working*
> *For those he loves the most*[35]

I didn't fully understand the gift that was my father until the last nine days of his life.

He was comatose when I arrived in Atlanta, unresponsive, not expected to survive the night. The family had gathered—my brother and his family, and Alice, Dad's beloved wife of three years, were all there. The doctor said it could be an hour or a day or a week. Dad had a living will—no extreme measures—it seemed so clear.

My brother had been on call most of the summer as Dad went from one medical emergency to another, so it was decided I would stay the night so my brother could go home and get some sleep. I'd call if anything happened.

Well, something did happen—a miracle. Dad woke up the next day, sat up, talked, wanted water, was himself. He was weak, couldn't speak above a whisper, couldn't really swallow, but was himself. We spoke frankly to him, told him how very ill he was, not likely to recover. He didn't believe us—classic denial, I thought, and for nine days, we settled into a new normal, me sleeping in his hospital room at night.

---

35. From "Silent Strong Dad" by Karen Boyer.

Whenever my brother or I mentioned that the end was near, he smiled, changed the subject, asked when Alice was coming.

On the eighth day two nurses helped him out of bed to sit in a chair. He wavered on the chair, bent over, shivering, his skinny body trembling at the effort to sit up.

"Do you want a blanket?" I asked.

"No," he rasped and smiled. "I've got my love to keep me warm." Alice. She arrived soon after, and I left them alone to hold hands and talk. It was all he wanted.

After Alice left, we settled into what had become our evening routine, watching television while he didn't eat. Happily, his team, the Atlanta Braves, was playing Cincinnati—playing Cincinnati and winning! Dad loved baseball and was happy that his team won, that Alice had spent the afternoon with him, and that I would be there through the night.

I woke with a start just after midnight. Too quiet in the room. Dad was dead. I called a nurse, called my brother, who came immediately, and we sat with him for the rest of the night, not saying much, but spending one more night in the love that never wore out.

𝒯𝒽𝑒 𝒰𝓁𝓉𝒾𝓂𝒶𝓉𝑒 𝒯𝒾𝓃𝓎 𝐻𝑜𝓊𝓈𝑒

My brother was a builder. He built things his whole life, towers of blocks, forts in the back yard, then decks, gazebos, houses, his own and others. He became a professional builder, and in his retirement he developed an active interest in the tiny house movement. He himself lived in 400 square feet—an apartment in his daughter's house, a house that was the first one he built more than forty years earlier, then, when she moved from that house to south Atlanta, he moved to a basement apartment next door.

He was always building something, but he didn't plan on his last project until he was diagnosed with stage 4 lung cancer in July of 2020. It was obvious that he would need what he called the ultimate tiny house—a coffin—sooner rather than later. A friend measured him for size, and he began construction using only repurposed wood.

❋

I found it hard to talk about that new project or even think about it until his daughter Jessamine posted a picture on Instagram of him sitting next to the finished coffin. "We are from a dry biting humor stock," she wrote, "and death and loss don't get a pass card."

Ah, yes, I thought. We *are* from a dry biting humor stock—that described both of my parents—her grandparents—and her father perfectly. He wasn't happy about the diagnosis, the death sentence, but he was a practical man who liked a project and got busy rather than complaining. As he pointed out, there is no stage 5.

He reminded me of our mother who said she was "Terrific!" every time I called her. She was "terrific" dragging an oxygen tank, "terrific" when she hardly had the energy to get out of bed. Her best option was to be "terrific." For my brother, building the ultimate tiny house was his version of "terrific."

Death was harder for our father to embrace, because he, the eternal optimist, didn't believe he was dying. He hadn't eaten in days and could barely keep his hospital gown over his shrunken body, so my brother and I told him. "Dad, we think this is the end."

He just shook his head. No, he had too much to live for.

The next day, I was alone with Dad when he motioned me over, "Bring me paper and pencil," he whispered conspiratorially. He took the pencil and sketched out his plan to escape from the hospital. I was to help him up on the food tray that stretched over his hospital bed, then quickly wheel him out the door, down the corridor to the elevator, down to the first floor, and out to my car.

"Don't say anything to anybody," he said.

"Dad, I can't do that," I said. "You are very sick."

He smiled his beatific smile, shook his head at the fairy tale I was spinning, explained the whole plan to me again, and was surprised when I refused, but not mad—he wasn't a man given to anger . . . and died the next night in that hospital bed.

When it was my brother's turn, he reminded me of the family tradition around death. Face it straight on with curiosity, but without complaint, like our mother and plan for the next stage, like our father, build the ultimate tiny house and take pride in the fact that the wood he used was repurposed—also part of our frugal Scotch upbringing. He researched and found an ecologically green cemetery, Milton Fields, 30 miles north of Atlanta, that would welcome his homemade coffin and unembalmed body.

He wasn't eager to enter that last tiny house, but as Jessamine ended an Instagram post, "Amongst the morbid humor, we hold hands along the path—and . . . we did discuss this wooden box will need to be stored, hopefully for quite a while unless he gets hit by a bus and then, you know, #fuckcancer."

✤

He didn't die that year. His oncologist changed his "miracle drug" and, with the initial help of steroids, he rebounded and was almost himself. Not as strong, not as energetic, but fully present, living his life, and with a coffin he had no immediate need for, that now would have to be stored, which wasn't possible in his basement apartment.

So he repurposed the coffin, stood it on the flat end, added three shelves and called it a bookcase. The bookcase served him well for another eighteen months, but when he entered hospice in late May of 2022, it was clear he would need the coffin for its original purpose. He removed the shelves, moved it to his bedroom, still standing on the flat end, and bought a life-sized plastic skeleton from Home Depot which he suspended in the upright coffin, lid open.

The sight of an open coffin with a skeleton in the bedroom of a dying man was mildly surprising to his family and friends, and startling to hospice nurses and technicians when they met him for the first time.

Lawana, his wonderful hospice nurse who visited twice a week, was accustomed to him and the skeleton in his coffin, and knew he would have a thoughtful answer when she asked what he wanted.

"A good death," he said.

※

Jessamine asked me to write his obituary. I asked his permission. "Well, okay," he said, "but it has to be funny."

Not that easy, but I tried, wrote two versions and showed them to him.

"Very nice," he said.

"Well done," he said.

"Do you mind if I have a go at it?" he said.

Of course not—it was his funeral, and his was the one we used.[36]

※

He also planned the funeral (and was adamant that it be called a funeral, *not* a memorial, service). He sent a detailed description of the service to family and to his many friends: he named the officiant, the pallbearers, specified the music he wanted—a bagpiper playing "*Going Home*" as the pallbearers brought the coffin forward, and a saxophonist at the end playing Coltane's "*I Wish I Knew*" as the coffin was lowered into the open grave. He bought heavy rope that he tested with the coffin to be sure it would bear the combined weight of coffin and body as it was lowered into the grave.

Maybe he comes off as controlling, but that was never my sense of him. A planner, yes, but a person who, like most of us, needed agency

---

36. When I told his daughters that the first sentence of the obituary was, "*Jeffrey Johnson is dead*"—*not* "died peacefully surrounded by family," etc., they laughed, because it was so *him*, direct and to the point. He said, ruefully, "Well, everyone will know I wrote it." Well, yes, what did he expect . . . and we posted it exactly as he wrote it.

over decisions that affected him directly. His detailed instructions were a true gift and enormously helpful to us all, family and friends.

After the service, our son Ahmed said he had never been to a funeral like that.

"None of us have," I said. It was a fitting tribute to a beloved man, even if he did plan it himself—or, perhaps, *because* he planned it himself.

One more thing: Lawana came to the funeral. Surely she doesn't attend the service for every hospice patient she cares for, but for my brother, she drove an hour through Atlanta traffic on her day off to witness the final chapter of a good death.

The Larger Circle

At the end of the memoir my mother wrote for our family, she said: "I remember examining Kathy when the small bundle was first laid in my arms . . . The most amazing thing I discovered was that her hands were tiny replicas of my own hands, even to the crook in the last joint of the middle fingers. And my hands are exactly like my mother's hands . . . I wonder if all this has something to do with what "life everlasting" really means.

Learning from the Young

Poet Wendell Berry in his poem "The Larger Circle" describes how we "clasp the hands of those that go before us/And the hands of those who come after us" and continues with the "larger circle of all creatures/Passing in and out of life . . ."

Berry's poem started me thinking about that ever-expanding circle of life after I interviewed my grandchildren in 2022, meeting with each individually to ask for their stories and opinions. I wanted to know how they describe their lives to themselves, and so I asked about their vision for the future, *their* future, a future I won't be around for. I interviewed these young people, ages sixteen to twenty-six at the time, because I was worried about their future, worried about the deep polarization in this country and in the world, worried about the climate—worried. I wondered what stories these beautiful young people were telling themselves . . . because the story we tell ourselves becomes the story we live.[37]

Well, they are worried too. Worried about the climate, the fate of our precious planet. "Climate change is a slow-moving calamity," one

---

37. When my brother was dying, my son Ahmed told me that "When we die, the book we read after death is the book of this life. We must do good now, so the book we read is good." Such a wise man.

said, "not happening fast enough to panic enough people, but reaching the point of no return." Another said that she may not have children because their future is so uncertain. They all mentioned the deep divide in the United States. "Why are we arguing about everything?" one asked.

Another spoke of his frustration with friends who won't even make space to talk, who find information that fits their view and stick to it. Another referred to Obama Care, as a time where both sides of the aisle acknowledged there was a large uninsured population—the disagreement was on *how* to fix it, not *if* it existed.

Why has that changed? How did we arrive at a time when there is repeated denial of facts, of science, of clear evidence? They all spoke of their own privilege, and of the racial divide, of the murder of George Floyd only a mile or so from their family homes. These are the stories they are living and telling themselves.

They are not the kind of the stories I was telling myself when I was twenty years-old. My grandchildren seem wiser than I was at their age . . . perhaps out of necessity?

What impressed me was the depth and breadth of their stories—from the immediate concerns and disappointments—a remote freshman year of high school, seeing friends only on a screen, a remote final year of college and no college graduation ceremony. One said it was hard to wake up and just turn on the computer—and school without interaction with friends was unrewarding.

And, as was both predictable and obvious, they all occupy the same bubble as their parents and grandparents. My goal—and effort—was not to ask leading questions, not what do you think about climate change or politics, but how to you see your future? What are you looking forward to? What worries you?

I asked for their stories because I was worried about the world I was leaving them, but also because I was curious. I wanted to know how all of this is going to turn out, I wanted to know how the next chapters of our collective story evolve, so I asked them—told them—to write to me when they turn seventy.

"I know I'll be dead," I said, "but I am *so* curious."

I will admit that I mentioned their writing to me more than once—okay, several times, because I *really* want them to do it. One granddaughter always says, "Nana, you're freaking me out."

But then her sister said, "Have you written to *your* grandmother? You should write to her!"

And suddenly my little story got bigger.

None of my four grandparents—all immigrants to the United States—ever flew in an airplane . . . or took a picture with their phone . . . or, for that matter, ever saw their parents or grandparents again after they got on that ship to cross the ocean. I, too, am part of a bigger story—we all are—and we need to be looking for it, embracing it, and, yes, celebrating it.

※

At the beginning of many public gatherings these days, the speaker begins by acknowledging the larger story, a story with parts that we have only recently understood and owned, that we are on stolen land, that our responsibilities extend both forward and backward, that these acknowledgements are an essential part of our story and, I believe, one of the gifts to ourselves.

The way we touch our history, the way we learn to understand it, the peaks and valleys, is through story. Oh, yes, we can list facts, dates, make a graph or a spreadsheet, but stories have power, leave an imprint, a memory, details, a deeper understanding. The stories we know, the stories we tell, the stories we understand and tell become the way we live.

Stories are the secret path . . . or tunnel . . . to comprehension and compassion. I say "secret" because they can easily be devalued, "oh, that's just a story" as in something made up, an entertainment, a yarn—but if it's a true story, a lived story, a **big** story, an inclusive story, it can help us understand, connect, and correct our own small vision of the world, and how we live in it.

Stories are multifaceted and also have trajectories, backward and forward. We call one the past, or history, the other the future, but they are all part of the same story. I can write to my grandparents and tell my grandchildren to write to me ... or to send me a TikTok video or whatever the next improbable manifestation of communication is available in the year 2070.

And now, thanks to the James Webb Space Telescope, we have seen that we truly are made of the stuff of stars, are part of "the larger circle of all creatures." We have been given a rare opportunity to open ourselves up to wonder, to awe, to revelation, to the beginning of ... time? ... existence? ... life? ... to cells that divide and divide and divide. We, all of us, are in that ever expanding dance and, although we can barely comprehend what we are looking at, the points of light, streaks of color, and that looming rocky image in the foreground are real, are here now—or there?—they existed 13 billion years ago—and we are looking at an earlier time!?

Really?

In another poem, Wendell Berry asked:

What banged?[38]

My question exactly.

And I would add: **Who** made it bang? Who set it in motion? What *is* it?

As I gawk at the James Webb images of creation in wonder and awe, the questions and mystery are still there—*What banged? How? Who? What do you call it? Is there a prime mover? God? Love?*

I don't know. But, for me, the power in those pictures from the Webb Telescope is that we are **all** there, the beginnings of all of us are there, of every creature that ever lived, of every bird, tree, mosquito, dinosaur and daisy, my grandparents and yours, today's children and their children to be. The gift of those amazing images is

---

38. *On the Theory of the Big Bang as the Origin of the Universe* by Wendell Berry.

connection—we are all there—the people and animals and trees and living creatures that we love, the ones we never knew, the neighbor it is hard to have a civil conversation with, and our best friend who agrees with us on everything. Some give a name to a prime mover, to the lighter of the fuse that set off the Big Bang—God is a fine word to use; also Mystery works; Spirit of Life; Creator; Light; Energy; Love.

We are all a miracle of love as is every other creature in the universe if you can define love as connection, as possibility, as belief in life, as faith in what comes next. We need to be willing to peer into the near and distant past, to see where we have come up short, acknowledge our wrongs, and celebrate our blessings; it's the only way we learn; it's the only way we see the whole story.

The time we live in, the stories we are living now, *are* challenging—there are the ones we all know about: the virus, polarization, climate change, the wars in Europe and the Middle East, and then there are our small, individual stories, some hopeful, some not—but in looking at the stories we tell ourselves I find enormous reservoirs of hope, particularly in the wonder of those images of the expanding universe ... and in my grandchildren, my particular future.

One said: "Politics is how you treat people." She went on to say, "I want to tell my grandchildren that their actions affect others. If everybody were vaccinated and quarantined when necessary, we wouldn't be beginning the third year of a pandemic. I like the image of a shared swimming pool," she said. "If we had all gotten out of the pool together, we could have cleaned it up. I've been waiting at the side of the pool for two years, and I'm getting fed up!"

The sixteen-year-old said (in early 2022, eleven days before Russia invaded Ukraine): "I have been following the issues in Ukraine closely and believe that if there is war between Russia and Ukraine, that will be more defining of this period in history than the pandemic. We remember World War I but hardly anybody knew about the Spanish flu until we were in another pandemic."

Another said she "wants a career that helps. It is better to act than to do nothing," and she's not giving up, "even if it makes sense to give up."

Another thanked me for the conversation, for the questions. I, of course, was grateful to them all for taking the time to meet with me... but in thinking about it later, I realized how important it is for us old people, so-called elders, to listen, to ask questions, to learn from the young. People my age know we need young people for help with our electronic devices, but asking questions of the young, questions we may have an answer for ourselves, but listening and learning, preferably without comment, except perhaps a nod of the head, is one way to find and understand the always evolving, bigger story.

That was the power of formalizing the conversation and calling it an interview. My job as interviewer was to listen and learn, to take notes, not to agree or disagree. That's not the goal or method of every conversation, but in those interviews, I am sure I heard more and learned more because *my* answer to the questions, my opinions, my biases or wishes for these young people I love never entered the conversation. I also interviewed their fifty-something parents and my eighty-five-year-old husband—many similar answers because we are all in the same bubble, but it was the conversation with these millennials that gave me hope, helped me understand and embrace the ever expanding story... and encouraged me to remind them that I *will* be looking for those letters when they turn 70... in 2072 or so.

And, yes, I have started my letter to my grandmother. She will be so glad.

Afterword

THE THIRD GOAL

I left for Peace Corps training the week I graduated from college, equipped with uninformed idealism and a BA in English. In other words, my few skills included the ability to write a decent sentence and the habit of losing myself in the sentences and paragraphs written by others.

Four years earlier, I had taken the memorable words of President Kennedy's inaugural address to heart: "Ask not what your country can do for you—ask what you can do for your country" and used that sentence as the first line of the essay on citizenship assigned by my high school English teacher. I don't remember if she told the class that our essays would be entered in a county-wide contest sponsored by local Civitan Clubs.

I do remember my surprise in winning first place in Hall County, getting my picture in the *Gainesville Times*, and then coming in second in the state-wide competition in Georgia. It was a thrill to win, but somehow felt inevitable because I had begun my essay with the inspiring words of our new president. In that address, Kennedy went on to speak to the rest of the world: "My fellow citizens of the world: ask not what America will do for you, but what together we can do for the freedom of man." In other words, we are in this together; let us do our best to create a world in which everybody thrives and cares for one another.

I was inspired to look up Kennedy's speech after seeing the list on Peace Corps Worldwide[39] of the 448 Peace Corps writers who have authored at least two books and imagining the several thousand books that list represents. I have always felt that the third goal of the Peace Corps was the most important: "To help promote a better understanding of other peoples on the part of Americans."

It is too common for we Americans to think we are the best or the smartest, most innovative, but those of us lucky enough to spend two or more years living and working in Ethiopia or Nepal or Ukraine know we are simply part of the great human adventure on earth, that there is more than one way to live and love and prosper, plan, hope, and suffer. That understanding is surely reflected in the thousands of books that list reflects. Telling a story, writing a poem, an essay, or a book helps increase knowledge, stimulate thought, and promote understanding and becomes a vital part of the radiating influence of the Peace Corps.

The other goals matter, of course. "To help the people of interested countries in meeting their need for trained men and women." The operable word for me is "interested." Peace Corps Volunteers don't rush in, uninvited, taking what we want, identifying what is broken and claiming we can fix it. That's colonialism. We are *invited* in to focus on a specific need. And, as Kennedy said, "If a free society cannot help the many who are poor, it cannot save the few who are rich."

The second goal: "To help promote a better understanding of Americans on the part of the peoples served" is also important, even though one of the first things I learned sixty years ago was that most Ethiopians already knew a lot about the United States. Even then, many years before the omnipresence of the internet, there were transistor radios in every town and village. The United States was big, powerful, and in the news every day. The effect of our presence as volunteers

---

39. https://peacecorpsworldwide.org/

was that local people got to know us, and we them, as human beings, ordinary, fallible, imperfect human beings.

But I always come back to the third goal: "to promote a better understanding of other people . . ." We volunteers are the people who benefited the most, who gained in understanding. When we settled into cities, towns, and villages around the world, we learned there is more than one way to live a good and generous life. "And so, my fellow Americans: ask not what your country can do for you—ask what you can do for your country." That's the Peace Corps I joined.

Rereading the inclusive words of President Kennedy assassinated more than sixty years ago gives me hope. Our country and the world are sorely divided now, but thousands of us have been transformed and educated by our Peace Corps experience. Volunteers returned to their posts after the worst of the pandemic; volunteers who will write more books, essays, poems; volunteers who will affirm directly or indirectly that we are one world, that we need each other. We speak different languages, eat different foods, have different practices and opinions, but we share this beautiful, fragile planet and must continue to learn, to see, and to listen to one another.

The Dragonfly

"Nana, do you want to get a tattoo with me." It was my 23-year-old granddaughter, Cailyn, calling.

Saying I was amazed by the invitation is an understatement. "What of?" I said.

"A dragonfly or . . ." Neither of us remember what the second choice was, perhaps because I said "Dragonfly!" so quickly, hardly pausing to consider that she was inviting me, 79-year-old me, to get a tattoo. The only possible answer when you are blessed with such an invitation from a grandchild is "Yes!"

On 2/22/22 (we all appreciate symmetry in numbers), Cailyn, her sister Sienna, and I got our tattoos, each different from the other. (Mine of course, features *two* dragonflies.)

Shortly after our adventure in the tattoo parlor, I came across a dragonfly sculpture which now hangs in my office and is the image that appears throughout *Married to Amazement*.

Acknowledgements

My deepest appreciation to the generous and talented staff at Mayfly Book Design and Publishing Services: Julie Scheife, owner and client services coordinator, book designer Mollie Mortimer and Creative Director Ryan Scheife. Their guidance, experience . . . and patience . . . were invaluable and much appreciated.

Thank you also to John Coyne who created Peace Corps Writers and Readers Worldwide 50 years ago--and to Marian Haley Beil who partnered with John to create the PC Writers Imprint that has supported and published 181 books by Peace Corps Volunteers who served in 144 countries around the world.

I have long envied John and Marian who were Ethi 1 Volunteers, in the first Peace Corps group to go to Ethiopia in 1962-64. Not only did their group meet with President Kennedy prior to their departure for Addis Ababa, but they were also welcomed, in person, by HIM, His Imperial Majesty Haile Selassie I, an honor and audience that was *not* repeated for the hundreds of us who followed in their footsteps.

Thank you to the following publications where some of these essays were first published, sometimes in a slightly different form.

"The Third Goal" in *Peace Corps Writers*, https://peacecorpsworldwide.org, 2023

"Return" in *Peace Corps Writers*, https://peacecorpsworldwide.org, 2021

"Teacher" in *Peace Corps Writers*, https://peacecorpsworldwide.org, 2021

"The Circus of the Damned" in *The Progressive*, October/November 2019

"Brighter Futures" in *Peace Corps Writers*, https://peacecorpsworldwide.org, 2008.

"Second Time Around" in *Peace Corps Writers*, https://peacecorpsworldwide.org, 2006.

"Proxy" in *Tanzania on Tuesday*, New Rivers Press, 1996.

"So This Is Paris" in *RPCV Writers and Readers*, 1994.

"Mwembe's Woman" in *Going Up Country*, Charles Scribner's Sons, 1994.

"Matatu" in *Going Up Country*, Charles Scribner's Sons, 1994.

Kathleen Coskran is a writer, teacher, and retired Principal of Lake Country School in Minneapolis. She served as a Peace Corps Volunteer in Ethiopia where she met her future husband, Chuck Coskran, also a Peace Corps Volunteer. After two years in Washington, D.C., they returned to east Africa where Chuck served as Deputy Director of the Peace Corps in Kenya. In 2006 they spent six months teaching at Zhejiang University in Hangzhou, China. She also volunteered for a month at Brighter Futures Children's Home, in Bistechap, Nepal, a village of 79 households southeast of Kathmandu. She posts her version of flash fiction on her blog, *Pocket Stories*, https://pocketstories-kcoskran.blogspot.com/2011/04/welcome.html and can be contacted through her web site, kathleencoskran.net.

Photo by Kris Berggren

www.ingramcontent.com/pod-product-compliance
Lightning Source LLC
Chambersburg PA
CBHW060519080526
44586CB00012B/544